D0622373

ONLY IN
SASKATCHEWAN

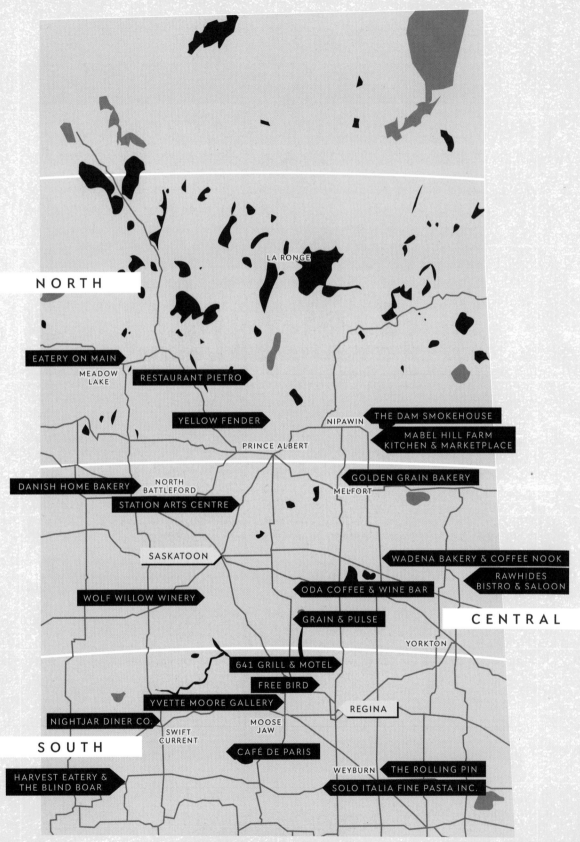

NORTH

EATERY ON MAIN

MEADOW LAKE

RESTAURANT PIETRO

YELLOW FENDER

NIPAWIN

THE DAM SMOKEHOUSE

MABEL HILL FARM KITCHEN & MARKETPLACE

PRINCE ALBERT

LA RONGE

DANISH HOME BAKERY

NORTH BATTLEFORD

STATION ARTS CENTRE

GOLDEN GRAIN BAKERY

MELFORT

SASKATOON

WADENA BAKERY & COFFEE NOOK

RAWHIDES BISTRO & SALOON

WOLF WILLOW WINERY

ODA COFFEE & WINE BAR

GRAIN & PULSE

CENTRAL

YORKTON

641 GRILL & MOTEL

FREE BIRD

YVETTE MOORE GALLERY

REGINA

NIGHTJAR DINER CO.

SWIFT CURRENT

MOOSE JAW

SOUTH

CAFÉ DE PARIS

WEYBURN

THE ROLLING PIN

HARVEST EATERY & THE BLIND BOAR

SOLO ITALIA FINE PASTA INC.

SASKATCHEWAN

SASKATOON

BABA'S HOMESTYLE PEROGIES

51ST ST E

WANUSKEWIN

16

CIRCLE DR

IDYLWYLD DR N

THE NIGHT OVEN BAKERY

BOTTÉ CHAI BAR

ODD COUPLE RESTAURANT

PICARO COCKTAILS & TACOS

COLLEGE DR

AYDEN KITCHEN & BAR

5

CALORIES RESTAURANT

GÜD EATS

BROADWAY

11

REGINA

CARAWAY GRILL

SIAM AUTHENTIC THAI RESTAURANT

VICTORIA AVE

CRAVE KITCHEN & WINE BAR

ITALIAN STAR DELI

TANGERINE

ALBERT ST

SKYE CAFÉ & BISTRO

WASCANA LAKE

HOUSTON PIZZA

HILL AVE

6

RING RD

ONLY IN SASKATCHEWAN

Recipes & Stories from
the Province's
Best-Loved Eateries

NAOMI HANSEN

PHOTOGRAPHY BY **GARRETT KENDEL**

TOUCHWOOD

Recipes copyright © 2022 by the individual contributor(s)
Selection, arrangement of recipes, and narrative text copyright © 2022 by Naomi Hansen
Photography copyright © 2022 by Garrett Kendel

All rights reserved. No part of this publication may be reproduced, stored in a retrieval system, or transmitted in any form or by any means, electronic, mechanical, photocopying, recording, or otherwise, without the prior written permission of the publisher. For more information, contact the publisher at:

TouchWood Editions
touchwoodeditions.com

The information in this book is true and complete to the best of the author's knowledge. All recommendations are made without guarantee on the part of the author or the publisher.

Edited by Lesley Cameron
Cover and interior design by Tree Abraham

Cataloguing data available from Library and Archives Canada
ISBN 9781771513555 (hardcover)
ISBN 9781771513562 (electronic)

TouchWood Editions acknowledges that the land on which we live and work is within the traditional territories of the Lkwungen (Esquimalt and Songhees), Malahat, Pacheedaht, Scia'new, T'Sou-ke and W̱SÁNEĆ (Pauquachin, Tsartlip, Tsawout, Tseycum) peoples.

We acknowledge the financial support of the Government of Canada through the Canada Book Fund, and the province of British Columbia through the Book Publishing Tax Credit.

This book was produced using FSC®-certified, acid-free papers, processed chlorine free, and printed with soya-based inks.

Printed in China.

26 25 24 23 22 1 2 3 4 5

To Paul,
Your unfailing support, encouragement, and love
make all of this possible.

Only in Saskatchewan was written, researched, and photographed in Treaty 4 and Treaty 6 territory, which are the traditional territories of the Cree, Saulteaux, Stoney, Dakota, Lakota, and Nakota, and the Homeland of the Métis Nation. I offer my respect and gratitude to the Indigenous peoples who have lived on this land for generations.

As a settler of this land, I acknowledge that I have much to learn from it. In the spirit of truth and reconciliation, it is with respect, humility, and reciprocity that I approach my writing about this place.

Contents

Introduction

The idea for this book came to me nearly five years ago while I was browsing in an Edmonton bookstore. Flipping through cookbooks in the food section, I stumbled upon *Edmonton Cooks: Signature Recipes from the City's Best Chefs* by Leanne Brown and Tina Faiz. "Hmm!" I thought. "Does Saskatchewan have something like this?" A quick search on my phone gave me the answer I was hoping for and, with that, I tucked the idea away in the back of my mind and left the store.

I have always been interested in cooking and baking, and, like many people, I have fond memories attached to food. As a child, my best days were those when my mom would whip up a batch of banana chocolate chip muffins or my baba would drop off a bag of freshly made cinnamon buns, still warm from the oven. Those treats were gone as quickly as they appeared, and I was invariably a key suspect in the recurring case of "Who Ate My Cinnamon Bun?", often at my little sister's expense. Years later, when I was living on my own for the first time, I gained an appreciation for just how much time, skill, and care goes into preparing fresh, quality food. I quickly realized the fruit plates my dad prepared each morning when I was growing up didn't just materialize out of thin air—although I confess I wished they did. After spending several weeks making and eating one single item for dinner in an attempt to save time—sweet potato fries one day, frozen salmon fillets the next—I realized this miserable pattern was not sustainable. I began to spend more and more time in the kitchen, and slowly but surely found my stride (and began to eat more balanced meals). I was pleasantly surprised by how much I enjoyed cooking, guided by a healthy mix of recipe-following and intuition.

As life carried on, the idea of writing this book was left to percolate in my mind. After graduating from university and finishing my job at the student newspaper, I launched a freelance writing and editing career in Saskatoon and dove into lifestyle writing, exploring topics like food, tourism, history, and the arts in Saskatchewan. Writing gave me a greater understanding of the province I call home and provided a front-row seat to local happenings, including the emerging food and culinary scene. It's no secret that in the last decade, Saskatchewan's food scene has undergone incredible growth. To quote Tracy Kelly-Wilcox of Grain & Pulse Bakery Café—who put it best when I interviewed her for this book—"It's been wonderful to see how the food scene has flourished, and to see the whole province waking up to what we have, what we do well, and to the producers who have been here all along." Her words certainly ring true, as Saskatchewan's emerging food and culinary scene has indeed evolved into an established one, putting the province on the map with the restaurants, bakeries, eateries, growers, farmers, and producers we have here in the Land of the Living Skies.

As I observed the changes happening in the culinary scene and the local food movement, the idea for this book began to gnaw at me. When I first approached TouchWood Editions with the idea, it was with a nervous optimism. To my great surprise and joy, an email from the publisher, Taryn Boyd, brought news I had only dreamed of. From there, we began to work together to construct and refine the concept—and then the real work began.

WHAT THIS BOOK IS ABOUT

Only in Saskatchewan shines a spotlight on the province's food and culinary landscape and is meant to serve two purposes. First and foremost, it presents a collection of recipes from restaurants, bakeries, cafés, and eateries province-wide. My goal is to provide you with a glimpse into the kitchens of some of Saskatchewan's most beloved establishments and allow you to recreate a little bit of that magic at home.

Second, this book showcases the people and places at the heart of Saskatchewan's food and culinary landscape, highlighting the talent, passion, and care behind the scenes. After visiting the places and talking with the people featured in these pages, I can personally attest to the fact that there are incredible things happening in Saskatchewan. I was consistently blown away by the commitment expressed by chefs and business owners to sourcing quality ingredients and taking an active role in the provincial food system. Their dedication is a testament to how Saskatchewan's hospitality and food production industries strengthen each other. Although terms like "local," "seasonal," and "farm-to-table" have become almost buzzwords in recent years, there are countless establishments that put in the time and effort required to bring these concepts to life. For this reason, you will see the word "local" a lot, but when I use that word, I simply mean that ingredients are sourced from within the province and, in many cases, from within a given community. In addition, the overarching theme throughout this book is that the recipes and restaurants featured are unique to the province, meaning that they are, quite literally, only in Saskatchewan.

HOW THIS BOOK WAS CREATED

I began writing this book in July 2020. Armed with an initial list of 80 possible establishments, I settled into what became six weeks of research. I combed through the online menus of every single restaurant, bakery, café, and eatery in Saskatchewan, and I even called tourist centres and town offices, pretending to be a prospective visitor, asking for recommendations for where to eat. I was not only looking for establishments that were known and loved by locals but also for those that were doing really innovative work in the kitchen. I wanted *Only in Saskatchewan* to offer a mix of both—all while honouring and reflecting the province's geographical and cultural diversity. Once I had finalized my list, I approached the selected establishments. Despite the ongoing COVID-19 pandemic, I was happy to find both excitement and encouragement in many of these conversations. From there, I worked with each participating establishment to decide on the featured recipes. In some cases, I knew I wanted to include a certain menu item right from the beginning because of its popularity, while other recipes were more collaborative choices. Many of the recipes also feature Saskatchewan-grown or produced ingredients, which was something I wanted to highlight throughout.

Along the way I was fortunate to convince Garrett Kendel of King Rose Visuals to join me in this project. After casually inquiring if he had experience with food photography (he did) and asking some vague questions about his availability for the upcoming year ("Sorry, what *is* this project?"), I finally let him in on the secret. Over a nine-month period we visited the featured establishments, meeting with chefs and business owners. It was important to me to photograph the recipes on site as much as possible, as I wanted the photos to include recognizable elements for Saskatchewanians. Whether it's the food, décor, or a familiar table setting, I hope you see an element or two that makes you stop and think "I've been there!" or "I've eaten that!"

Of course, unlike most home cooks, eating establishments are not cooking for four to six people, so we collaborated on adapting—and testing—the recipes to scale them down. I've also made a point of including and labelling wheat-free and plant-based recipes (gluten-free and vegan readers, I see you!), and made notes about where you can substitute or omit an ingredient to make a recipe gluten-free or vegan. Near the back of the book, you will find a Sourcing Local Guide (page 278), which I've prepared to help you track down ingredients that are available only seasonally or may be challenging to find.

It is important to note that the list of establishments featured in *Only in Saskatchewan* is by no means exhaustive. It would be impossible to include all of the best-loved spots in every single Saskatchewan city, town, and village, because there are simply too many (not a bad problem to have!). The provincial landscape is dotted with many a beloved spot, and so I offer this book as a glimpse of Saskatchewan's food and culinary scene—a piece of the pie, if you will.

THE COVID-19 PANDEMIC

I would be remiss not to mention that *Only in Saskatchewan* was completed entirely during the COVID-19 pandemic. It is with great humility and gratitude that I extend a thank you to all the participating establishments for their contributions and time, knowing that the pandemic was not kind to many industries, but that the hospitality industry suffered particularly badly. COVID -19 presented challenges in writing this book, not only on my end, but for the participating chefs and business owners, who were making sense of changing restrictions and the general uncertainty of running a business during a pandemic.

When I first began the process of contacting establishments, I had hoped to feature a total of 50. In the end, for various reasons, the final count came in at less than that. Unfortunately, a few of the spots I wanted to include closed permanently due to the pandemic, while others chose not to participate due to the unpredictability of the times. For this reason, there are a few geographical gaps that otherwise would have been filled. Had this book been written under other circumstances, the end result would likely have been different—much longer, for one thing.

With this in mind, as we all emerge weary and changed from the shared experience of the COVID-19 pandemic, it has never been more important to support our provincial establishments and food systems. The establishments featured in these pages are more than just restaurants, cafés, and bakeries. They are places that facilitate connection and hold both memories and history. They are places where personal and communal identities are built and where people are drawn together, all around a common unifier: food. Supporting the food and culinary scene is a fundamental piece of rebuilding our post-pandemic world. To thrive collectively, we must support and lean on each other, and there is no better place to begin than within our own communities.

AN EXTRAORDINARY JOURNEY

The process of writing *Only in Saskatchewan* was an extraordinary journey, both figuratively and literally, as I had the chance to visit corners of the province I had not been to previously. To have the opportunity to explore the food scene in such depth was truly an honour and something I do not take lightly. As an avid foodie, I love to eat out and try new places, and admittedly, I'm *that person* who needs to take a photo of their plate before digging in. On any given Sunday, I can usually be found in the kitchen doing meal prep and baking for the week. I find stability in the act of following a recipe to produce predictable results, but I also find creativity in combining ingredients just to see what happens. For the record, my experiments *usually* work, with a few exceptions (don't ask my husband about the time I tried a falafel bowl with peanut sauce—he will not let that one go). Mishaps aside, the kitchen is often a place where I come to understand myself a little bit better, knowing that allowing curiosity to take the reins regularly is good for the soul. As I wrote *Only in Saskatchewan*, it took shape as a project that bridged two things I enjoy dearly: cooking and dining out. In a sense, this book is very much a meeting point, a place where kitchens and eateries collide.

It is my sincere wish that you will find a new favourite recipe, a staple you'll make time and time again. Likewise, once you've recreated these dishes in your own kitchen, I hope you feel inspired to hit the road and visit the featured spots. Saskatchewanians are no strangers to driving long hours—I'd venture to say we even enjoy it—and I encourage you to visit an establishment new to you. Make an excursion for dessert, turn lunch into a day trip, or drive farther than usual for dinnertime.

As you read and look through *Only in Saskatchewan*, I hope you find joy, wonder, and familiarity in its pages, and I hope you feel a genuine sense of pride for this beautiful, diverse, and dynamic province we call home.
—Naomi

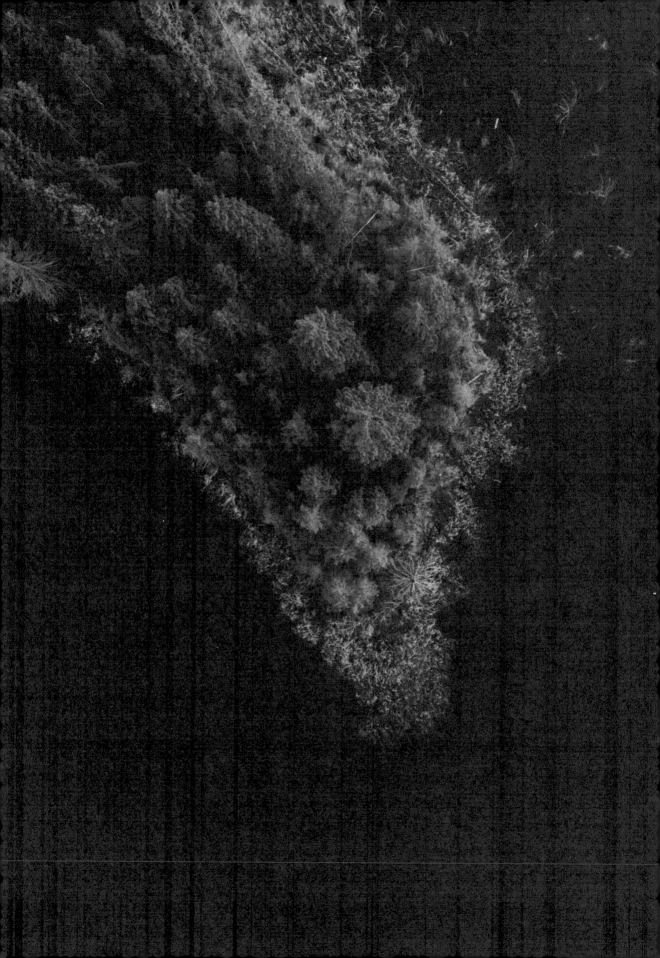

North

—

Mabel Hill's Bourbon Brown Butter Cake with Sour Cherry Topping
and Hot Sour Cream Glaze × **19**

Mabel Hill's North SK Spruce Cocktail × **21**

The Dam Smokehouse's Jerk Pork Belly × **27**

Yellow Fender's Autumn Apple and Cheddar Scones
with Rosemary Pepper Butter × **33**

Eatery on Main's Ferrero Rocher Cheesecake × **39**

Restaurant Pietro's Tableside Caesar Salad × **45**

Restaurant Pietro's Saskatoon Berry Iced Tea × **47**

Northern Saskatchewan is vast and varied, home to boreal forest and an abundance of natural beauty. Many of the locations featured in this chapter are surrounded by such beauty, from northern flora to picturesque lakes. The north always brings nature to the forefront of my mind, particularly the ways we connect with nature through the changing seasons and, in turn, how we connect with the seasons through food.

For me, summers past have often included camping trips to northern Saskatchewan, with days spent exploring the ins and outs of provincial and national parks. When I was growing up, family camping trips were especially memorable, and typically began with a jam-packed minivan and a heated exchange about over-packing tendencies. Once we hit the road, heading north on Highway 11, out came the snacks and CDs. In just a few short hours, the landscape transformed from golden prairie to tall, looming evergreens, which framed the outstretched highway for kilometres on end.

Often, camping memories include weather-related incidents, like the time someone—we're still not sure who—left the tent flaps open when we went to get ice cream and it started pouring. Beyond amusing mishaps— which are only amusing in hindsight, of course—camping and spending time in nature always reminds me to slow down and savour the simple things. Given the speed of life, sometimes slowing down feels rebellious. When I deliberately unplug from the constant distractions of modern life, I'm often surprised at the quiet that ensues, and I'll find myself observing things I otherwise would have missed. There's suddenly space to notice the mesmerizing flames of a dancing fire, and time to linger and watch the sun set as the cool night air blows in. A change of pace is a natural prompt to take some time for reflection, which is why I'll always think of summers in the north as easygoing, formative times.

Being in nature also provides the welcome chance to connect with our food and where it comes from. If you've ever spent time on the lake fishing, you'll know the pure delight that comes from feeling a tug on your line. That tug means the odds of enjoying freshly caught fish for dinner, grilled over an open flame or pan-fried with a crispy coating, are certainly in your favour.

Then there's berry picking. When I was growing up, my family spent many a hot summer day gathering strawberries, Saskatoon berries, and raspberries. After throwing on old clothes, we'd head out to our destination, empty buckets in tow. Under the scorching sun the endless rows of berries would be waiting, warm to the touch. As we navigated the bushes, we'd fill our pails with ripe fruit, our faces prickling with heat and knees caked in dirt. Whenever I happened upon the perfect berry, I simply had to pop it in my mouth—nothing compares to a plump, freshly picked berry, bursting with juice. At day's end, with bellies full of berries and a trunk full of heavy pails, we'd head home to begin the process of washing and freezing our harvest. Later on, my mom would use the berries for jam, smoothies, and desserts like homemade ice cream or fruit crisp.

Experiencing food in accordance with the changing seasons is a process to relish, and allows us to connect with the natural world. Many establishments province-wide look to the intrinsic link between food and nature for inspiration in the kitchen, working alongside the rhythm of Saskatchewan's seasons. It's a practice that can be grounding—after all, nature is never in a rush, and its predictability is constant, season after season, year after year.

MABEL HILL FARM KITCHEN & MARKETPLACE

SW 2-51-14-W2 RM of
Nipawin #487
Nipawin, SK S0E 1E0
(306) 862-2040
mabelhill.com

Mabel Hill is a destination that feels entirely Saskatchewan, offering a dining experience that embodies farm-to-table in a unique way. Owner and chef Michael Brownlee fondly remembers spending summers working on his grandparents' fruit and vegetable farm, and says it showed him how farming can bring families together. He wanted to recreate that experience at Mabel Hill, where guests can dine right beside the garden where much of the restaurant's produce is grown.

The farmhouse-inspired restaurant is striking inside, with tall ceilings and wood beams that make it feel spacious and grand. Details like industrial chandeliers and a wood-burning stove provide rustic character, while an open kitchen gives diners a glimpse behind the scenes. A wraparound porch doubles as a patio in warmer months and offers scenic views, including evergreen trees and flax and canola fields, which come alive with soft lilac and bright yellow in summer. Mabel Hill also has an on-site marketplace where they sell local goods, a firepit where you can enjoy a post-dinner campfire, and a stunning event venue complete with a gazebo perched atop Mabel Hill, for which the site is named.

If that wasn't enough, the food at Mabel Hill is exceptional. Originally from Carrot River, Michael trained at the Culinary Institute of Canada and later worked as sous chef at Ayden Kitchen & Bar in Saskatoon. His passion for quality ingredients shines through in his menu, and he can often be found wandering over to the garden to pick produce for dinner. The menu changes with the seasons but focuses on big-city eats in a relaxed country setting. Think bison tartare, fresh oysters, and handmade pasta, but with a post-meal stroll through the garden and a visit to their marketplace to pick up homemade jam afterwards—that's Mabel Hill in a nutshell.

Mabel Hill's Bourbon Brown Butter Cake with Sour Cherry Topping and Hot Sour Cream Glaze

—

» MAKES 6–9 SERVINGS
» TIME: 2 HOURS

Hot Sour Cream Glaze

1 (11 oz/300 mL) can of sweetened condensed milk*

½ cup full-fat sour cream

2 Tbsp whipping (35%) cream

Bourbon Brown Butter Cake

½ cup granulated sugar

½ cup packed brown sugar

2 eggs

1 Tbsp vegetable oil

1½ tsp vanilla extract

½ tsp sea salt

½ tsp baking powder

½ cup buttermilk

2 oz bourbon

1½ cups all-purpose flour

½ cup unsalted butter

Sour Cherry Topping

4 cups fresh or frozen pitted sour (tart) cherries**

2 cups granulated sugar

2 Tbsp freshly squeezed lemon juice

3 Tbsp cornstarch

3 Tbsp water

This recipe feels festive and features big, bold flavours, making it a crowd-pleaser for special gatherings. The hot sour cream glaze combines the soft caramel notes of dulce de leche with sour cream, creating a rich, smooth cream cheese flavour. Michael sources sour cherries locally for the sour cherry topping, which adds sweetness and a pop of colour to the warm bourbon brown butter cake. To split up the preparation, you can make the cake and sour cherry topping ahead of time, or buy a can of dulce de leche for the glaze.

HOT SOUR CREAM GLAZE

1. About 1 hour before you begin to prepare the cake, start on the dulce de leche for the glaze. If you are using a premade version of dulce de leche, you can skip this step.
2. Fill a medium saucepan with water and submerge the can of sweetened condensed milk (unopened) in the water.
3. Allow it to simmer, covered, on medium-high heat for about 1½ hours. You might have to top up the water now and again.
4. Using tongs, remove the can from the water and allow it to cool completely before opening. The milk should have turned a light amber colour similar to caramel. Set it aside in the fridge until you are ready to assemble and serve the cake.

BOURBON BROWN BUTTER CAKE

1. While the condensed milk is bubbling away, bake the cake.
2. Preheat the oven to 325°F (165°C). Line the bottom of an 8- × 8-inch cake pan with parchment paper and spray the bottom and sides with cooking spray.
3. Place both sugars, the eggs, oil, vanilla, salt, and baking powder in a large mixing bowl. Whisk by hand until well combined.
4. Add the buttermilk and bourbon, and whisk again until smooth.
5. Gradually whisk the flour into the mixture ½ a cup at a time. You want to eliminate any lumps, but be careful not to over mix.
6. Place the butter in a small saucepan over medium heat and cook until it starts to foam and brown, 5–8 minutes. Remove from the heat and gently fold the warm melted butter into the cake batter with a spatula until fully incorporated.
7. Pour the cake batter into the prepared cake pan and bake on the centre rack of the oven until a cake tester comes out clean when inserted into the centre, about 25 minutes.
8. While the cake is baking, prepare the sour cherry topping (below).

9. Remove the cake from the oven and allow it to cool slightly while you assemble the glaze and get ready to serve (below).

SOUR CHERRY TOPPING

1. Place the cherries, sugar, and lemon juice in a medium saucepan over medium heat. Stir together to combine and bring to a simmer. Keep at a simmer until the mixture is hot and the cherries are cooked through, about 10 minutes.
2. Whisk together the cornstarch and water in a small bowl. Stir into the cherry mixture to combine. Simmer until the mixture thickens, 2 more minutes.
3. Remove from the heat and allow it to cool at room temperature.

TO ASSEMBLE

1. To assemble the glaze, place the dulce de leche, sour cream, and whipping cream in a small saucepan, and stir to combine.
2. Bring it to a simmer over medium heat, stirring occasionally, and then immediately remove from the heat. The glaze needs to be used while it's still warm and before it starts to firm up, so timing is everything!
3. Cut the still warm cake into 6 or 9 pieces and arrange the pieces in individual bowls or on plates. Add a generous spoonful of hot sour cream glaze over each portion.
4. Serve the cake immediately with a side of the sour cherry topping in a small dish or ramekin, or drizzle it on top of the warm cake.

*The can of sweetened condensed milk is used to make dulce de leche for the glaze. It can be substituted with a premade version of dulce de leche, if desired.

**If sour (tart) cherries are not available or in season, you can substitute them with the same volume of sweet cherries. They'll make the topping slightly sweeter, but not so much that you'll need to add less sugar.

Tip: You can make the cake and topping ahead of time, and let them both cool completely before you plan to serve the dessert. The cake is best served warm, so if you prepare it in advance, be sure to heat it up prior to serving. Preheat the oven to 350°F (175°C) and line a rimmed baking sheet with parchment paper. Cut the cake into 6 or 9 pieces and place the pieces on the baking sheet, evenly spaced. Then warm the cake for 5 minutes in the oven while you assemble the glaze. Serve immediately.

Sourcing tip: For where to find sour (tart) cherries, see the Sourcing Local Guide (page 291).

Mabel Hill's North SK Spruce Cocktail

—

Caramelized Spruce Tip Syrup

4 cups packed spruce tips, fresh or thawed*

2 cups granulated sugar

2 cups water

North SK Spruce Cocktail

1½ oz Stumbletown Rock N' Rye**

½ oz Stumbletown Maté Amaro**

1½ tsp caramelized spruce tip syrup (above)

2 dashes Angostura bitters

Ice cubes

1 boozy cherry, for garnish (maraschino works well)

1 piece of orange peel, for garnish

This cocktail tastes like an evergreen forest in a glass, with a sharp, earthy flavour and subtle notes of citrus from the spruce tips. A bright green colour, spruce tips are the new shoots of a tree, and Mabel Hill sources them directly from their farmyard for this cocktail. You can buy spruce tips from specialty retailers or forage them when they're in season, which is late May or early June in Saskatchewan. Fresh spruce tips can be refrigerated in an airtight container for up to 1 month. If you have leftover syrup, try drizzling it on pancakes or ice cream. Note that you have to let the syrup steep overnight before you can use it.

CARAMELIZED SPRUCE TIP SYRUP

1. Place the spruce tips and sugar in a food processor or blender, and blend on high speed until well combined.
2. Transfer to a medium saucepan. Add the water and bring to a rolling boil, undisturbed, on high heat. Boil for 2 minutes and then remove from the heat.
3. Let the mixture sit, uncovered, for 10 minutes on the counter to cool slightly. Then cover it with plastic wrap, or transfer to an airtight container, and allow it to sit on the counter to steep overnight.
4. The next day, strain the syrup through a fine-mesh sieve into a medium saucepan. You may have to press on the mixture with the back of a spoon to release all the liquid.
5. Cook the syrup, uncovered, on medium heat, stirring regularly, until the mixture resembles a honey consistency and is dark amber in colour, 20 to 40 minutes. The syrup will start to turn amber after 20 to 25 minutes, but cooking it longer will result in a deeper colour and flavour and a thicker syrup. Cooking times may vary depending on the saucepan and stove, but note that the syrup will continue to thicken as it cools. If the syrup is too thick once cooled, you can add it back to the saucepan with a bit more water (start with 1 Tbsp) and reheat it to thin it out.
6. Once the desired consistency is reached, remove from the heat and let cool completely in the saucepan at room temperature.
7. Store the cooled syrup in an airtight container in a cool, dark place for up to 3 months. If it hardens, you can simply heat it up again on the stove or microwave it for 20–30 seconds to thin it out prior to using.

NORTH SK SPRUCE COCKTAIL

1. Place the rye, amaro, syrup, bitters, and a scoop of ice cubes in a mixing glass or cocktail shaker. Using a spoon, stir the cocktail for 30 seconds, or using a cocktail shaker, shake hard for 30 seconds.
2. Place 1 or 2 ice cubes in a short rocks glass.
3. Strain the cocktail through a cocktail strainer or a small sieve into the rocks glass.
4. Add a boozy cherry and a piece of orange peel for garnish. Serve immediately.

*If you have frozen spruce tips, thaw them overnight in the fridge prior to starting the recipe. Note that freeze-dried spruce tips will not work for this recipe, as they lack moisture and will simply absorb all of the water.

**Mabel Hill uses Rock N' Rye and Maté Amaro from Stumbletown Distilling in Saskatoon. Although you can substitute another brand of rye or amaro in this recipe, I recommend using Stumbletown's products. Their Rock N' Rye is a unique cherry old-fashioned-style product, using Saskatchewan-grown sour cherries, rock sugar simple syrup, dehydrated fruit, and infused botanicals. Other ryes typically don't contain fruit and are unsweetened, so for an authentic version of this cocktail be sure to try it with Stumbletown's spirits.

Tip: At Mabel Hill, this cocktail is served with a spruce tip ice cube. Simply add a couple spruce tips with water to an ice cube tray and freeze.

Sourcing tip: For where to find spruce tips and Stumbletown Distilling products, see the Sourcing Local Guide (page 292).

THE DAM SMOKEHOUSE

206 1st Avenue West
Nipawin, SK S0E 1E0
(306) 862-3617
facebook.com/dam-
smokedamgood

The Dam Smokehouse offers something you don't see every day: smokey Southern BBQ on the Canadian Prairies. Owner Faron Saufert first fell in love with Southern BBQ during a trip to St. Louis. He'd always dreamed of opening a restaurant, and, after working in agriculture for 20 years, one day he decided he was going to make it happen. The rest, he says, is history.

Having never smoked a piece of meat before, he spent the weeks prior to opening in 2017 perfecting staples like brisket, ribs, and BBQ sauce. Although he might have faced an initial learning curve, nowadays it's clear that Faron has honed his art. Customers regularly visit from across the province and beyond, some even driving upwards of five hours for a meal.

When you walk into the Dam Smokehouse, mouth-watering smells of smokey, woody barbeque hit you immediately. But don't be distracted by the smells. Look up and you'll see old records, donated by the community, lining the entire ceiling. The décor has a relaxed, rustic feel, with Mason jar lights overhead and old licence plates and signs on the walls. A stuffed wild boar hangs above one of the wooden booths, which are perfect for groups.

Faron sources ingredients locally as much as possible, including his house sausage, from the Outback Butcher in Carrot River, and pork from Pine View Farms, outside of Saskatoon. The drinks menu also exclusively features Saskatchewan-made spirits and craft beer. The chalkboard menu changes regularly, offering everything from pulled pork, roast chicken, and bison ribs to sides like cornbread and house-made Caesar salad. Faron prides himself on offering fresh food cooked to perfection, and it's a model that's earned the Dam Smokehouse a strong reputation. After all, if you have customers driving hours for a meal, I'd say you're definitely doing something right.

The Dam Smokehouse's Jerk Pork Belly

—

» MAKES 10–12 SERVINGS
» TIME: 6½ HOURS +
  48 HOURS TO MARINATE
» GLUTEN-FREE (OPTION)

Jerk Marinade

12 Scotch bonnet peppers,
  stems removed*
2 large white onions, diced
  small
2 garlic bulbs, chopped
1 bunch green onions, diced
  small
2½ Tbsp Chinese five-spice
  powder
2½ Tbsp allspice
2 Tbsp coarse ground black
  pepper
1 Tbsp ground mace or
  nutmeg
1 Tbsp kosher salt or sea salt
2 tsp dried thyme leaves
2 cups soy sauce or low-
  sodium soy sauce (gluten-
  free if preferred)
½ cup olive oil

Pork Belly

1 (5 lb) pork belly, skin
  removed
1–2 chunks or sticks of
  apple or hickory wood, for
  smoking
1–2 limes, cut into wedges,
  for garnish

This pork belly is cooked slowly on low heat, making it incredibly tender. The layers of soft, flavourful fat and plump, juicy meat pull apart so easily you barely have to cut it. Faron recommends looking for pork belly at your local butcher shop to ensure you get a cut with an even balance of meat and fat. To contrast the rich flavour, pair this dish with grilled or roasted vegetables like Brussels sprouts, zucchini, or asparagus. The jerk marinade can also be used for other dishes like chicken wings or thighs—cook them over hot coals or grill them over an open flame for best results. Note that the meat has to marinate for 48 hours.

JERK MARINADE

1. Place all the marinade ingredients in a blender or food processor. Blend on medium to high speed until the mixture is smooth and fragrant and is an earthy brown colour.

PORK BELLY

1. Place the pork belly on a rimmed baking sheet. Using a very sharp knife, make a series of scores, each about ¼-inch deep, across the entire slab of meat. Repeat in the other direction to form a diamond pattern. Turn the pork belly over and score the other side in the same way. Scoring allows the marinade to work deeper into the meat and results in better flavour.
2. Rub half of the marinade into the pork belly, working it in from top to bottom with your hands, until the meat is covered evenly on both sides. Be sure to apply marinade to the grooves you cut. Cover the rimmed baking sheet tightly with plastic wrap and place it in the fridge to marinate for 48 hours. Transfer the other half of the marinade to an airtight container and refrigerate until needed.
3. Preheat a smoker to 230°F (110°C) or the oven to 250°F (120°C). If you're using a smoker, place the wood chunks on top of the hot coals. You should see a faint white wisp of smoke. If there is any black or heavy smoke, wait until it is white, otherwise you will not get a clean burn on the wood. If you're using the oven, line a rimmed baking sheet with aluminum foil.
4. Remove the plastic wrap from the pork and place the pork belly fat side up in the smoker, or fat side up on the prepared baking sheet in the oven. Cook the pork belly in the smoker or oven until it reaches an internal temperature of 165°F (75°C), 5–6 hours. If you're using an oven, the pork belly may begin to char slightly on top after a while, so, if needed, place a sheet of aluminum foil

overtop of the pork belly for the remainder of the cooking time. Once it's done, the fat should begin to render away, but the meat will still be firm enough to cut. If the internal temperature is higher than 165°F (75°C), this is perfectly fine; it will just result in more of the fat being rendered away.

5. Remove the pork belly from the smoker or oven. Using a silicone barbeque brush or a spoon, spread the reserved marinade on the top and sides of the meat, being sure to cover it evenly. Cut the pork belly into 10–12 portions and serve immediately with a lime wedge for garnish.

*Scotch bonnet peppers can be difficult to find and can be substituted with 12 habanero or Thai chili peppers, with the stems removed. You can also use fewer peppers if you want a milder, less spicy version of this recipe.

Sourcing tip: For where to find pork belly, see the Sourcing Local Guide (page 290).

YELLOW FENDER

Yellow Fender has been a pillar in the Christopher Lake community for over two decades. The business has been run by three successive generations of women, all of whom love to be creative in the kitchen.

Connie Freedy and her daughter, Heidi O'Brodovich, started Yellow Fender as a catering business in 2001 and established the restaurant in 2004. Connie grew up on a farm in the Cut Knife area and began cooking at an early age, helping with baking and preserving. She always wanted to cook professionally, so as an adult, she went back to school and became a Red Seal chef. Heidi also spent part of her childhood on a farm, near Holbein, and both women credit their connection to farming as fundamental to how they approach food: they respect the seasons and always focus on made-from-scratch food, using real ingredients. Heidi notes they almost never make the same thing twice, creating new treats depending on what's available.

Heidi's daughter, Emily White, grew up with the business and fondly recalls making mud pies behind the restaurant as a kid. Since then, she has traded mud pies for real ones and worked many summers at Yellow Fender. In 2019, she won gold in the Skills Canada provincial baking competition and then competed nationally in Halifax, indicating she's definitely inherited her family's talent in the kitchen.

After nearly 17 years of operating the restaurant, Connie and Heidi sold the building that housed Yellow Fender in the spring of 2021. Although the restaurant portion is now closed, Heidi notes that the Yellow Fender legacy will continue on in one form or another. With a long-standing connection to the community through homemade food, Yellow Fender's strength lies in the women behind it, who dare to dream what a touch of imagination can do.

Yellow Fender's Autumn Apple and Cheddar Scones with Rosemary Pepper Butter

—

» MAKES 8–12 SCONES + 1 CUP BUTTER
» TIME: 1 HOUR 30 MINUTES

Autumn Apple and Cheddar Scones

1½ cups + 1 Tbsp unbleached white or all-purpose flour

1½ cups + 1 Tbsp pastry flour

3½ Tbsp granulated sugar

3 Tbsp + 2 tsp baking powder

1 tsp sea salt

⅔ cup salted butter, chilled and cubed

1¾ cups shredded or crumbled sharp cheddar cheese (white or orange)

1½ cups medium-diced fresh apple (about 2 medium-size apples, skin on or removed)*

1 large egg

3–4 Tbsp whole milk or half-and-half (10%) cream

Topping

2–3 Tbsp whole milk or half-and-half (10%) cream

⅓ cup shredded or crumbled sharp cheddar cheese (white or orange)

Rosemary Pepper Butter

1 cup salted butter, softened and cubed

½ tsp cracked black pepper

½ tsp chopped fresh rosemary leaves

Yellow Fender's scones came in both sweet and savoury flavours, including lemon cream, Saskatoon berry, and, of course, apple and cheddar. This recipe is by Connie, Heidi, and Emily, who all worked together to refine it, and it's the perfect excuse to use up fresh apples in autumn if you find yourself with a surplus. For a tasty variation, try adding cooked and crumbled bacon to the recipe (6 strips per batch should do the trick!) or substitute pear and Parmesan cheese for the apple and cheddar. Leftover rosemary pepper butter works wonderfully on potatoes or fresh bread, or can be used when cooking a variety of ingredients to add a deliciously aromatic touch.

AUTUMN APPLE AND CHEDDAR SCONES AND TOPPING

1. Preheat the oven to 400°F (200°C). Line a baking sheet with parchment paper.
2. Sift both flours prior to measuring. Place both flours, the sugar, baking powder, and salt in a large bowl. Stir together to combine.
3. Cut the chilled butter into the flour mixture, either with a pastry cutter or by combining the flour mixture with the butter in a food processor and pulsing until the mixture is crumbly and pea-sized pieces of butter are visible. If the butter warms up too much during this process, you can refrigerate the mixture for 5–10 minutes. If you're using a food processor, transfer the mixture back to the bowl when done.
4. Add the cheese and apples to the bowl, and gently stir to combine with the flour and butter.
5. Whisk together the egg and 3 Tbsp of the milk in a small bowl, and then slowly add it to the dry mixture in two additions, kneading with your hands in between each addition. The dough should begin to come together while maintaining a strand-like, shaggy texture, which will ensure a tender final product. If needed, add the remaining 1 Tbsp of milk to reach the desired consistency. Be careful not to overwork the dough, as this will make the scones tough.
6. Lightly flour a clean surface and place the dough on it. Knead the dough four to six times, until it forms a slightly sticky consistency. It should not be so sticky that it gets stuck to your hands, so, if necessary, add a little bit more flour to reach the desired consistency.
7. Shape the dough into a large flat disk, about 2 inches thick, and cut it into 8 evenly sized triangles (almost as if you were cutting a pizza). If you want slightly smaller scones, you can shape the

dough into 2 flat disks, each about 2 inches thick, and cut each of them into 6 triangles. Keep the disks together after cutting; the scones should not be separated yet.

8. For the topping, brush 2–3 Tbsp of milk on top of the entire disk(s) and then sprinkle the ⅓ cup of shredded cheddar cheese evenly on top. You may need to gently press the cheese into the dough to ensure it sticks.

9. Transfer the scones to the baking sheet and separate them, spacing them about 1 inch apart from each other. You may need two baking sheets. Let them rest for 5 minutes before they go into the oven.

10. Bake the scones on the centre rack of the oven if using one pan or on two racks if using two pans. The larger scones bake for 20–25 minutes, and the smaller scones bake for 15–20 minutes. If you are using two pans, place one on the top rack and one on the bottom and rotate them at the halfway point. The scones are done when a toothpick or cake tester inserted in the centre of a scone comes out clean.

11. Transfer the scones to a cooling rack and let cool for about 5 minutes. Serve warm with rosemary pepper butter on the side.

ROSEMARY PEPPER BUTTER

1. Place the butter, pepper, and rosemary in a medium bowl. Using a handheld electric mixer, beat on medium speed until the butter is smooth and well combined. If you want a bolder flavour, increase the pepper and rosemary to ¾ tsp each, or to taste.

2. Transfer the butter to a small dish and serve immediately with the scones.

*Yellow Fender uses homegrown September Ruby apples for this recipe. In the off-season, you can use Granny Smith, Royal Gala, or your favourite variety, depending on the level of tartness you prefer. This recipe works best with fresh apples, as frozen will produce too much moisture and the scones won't bake up as well.

Tip: For sage pepper butter, substitute the rosemary with ½ tsp chopped fresh sage leaves.

226 Centre Street
Meadow Lake, SK S9X 1L2
(306) 236-8864
eatonmain.com

EATERY ON MAIN

Eatery on Main is a not-so-hidden gem in Meadow Lake's downtown, serving as both a community spot and the go-to place to eat and drink. It's a beautifully decorated space that owner Kassidy Dunsing calls a home away from home because of its friendly and relaxed atmosphere. The interior is bright and inviting, with inspirational quotes posted on the walls and fun, retro music playing overhead. Large wooden booths line the front windows, and red brick runs along the main counter where their motto, "Eat Real, Eat Local, Eat on Main," is proudly displayed.

Eatery on Main opened in 2012, and Kassidy bought the business in 2018. When she took over, she wanted to update the restaurant by giving it a pub-like feel, adding features like appetizers and a cocktail menu. From 8 AM to 4 PM, breakfast and lunch customers head to the front counter to order, and from 4 PM until closing, the restaurant operates like a pub, with table service both inside and outside on their patio in warmer months. The menu features favourites like their mouth-watering homemade burgers and decadent cheesecakes, two items they're known for locally. There are plenty of gluten-free and vegetarian options on the menu too, like their gluten-free scones and the falafel burger (my personal favourite!), which is served with avocado and fresh tzatziki.

Kassidy is passionate about doing random acts of kindness, and one of her key business priorities is community service, including initiatives like food drives and a city-wide garbage clean-up each spring. She often partners with other businesses in Meadow Lake to support and advocate for each other, too. It's an approach that helps build connection within the local community and, in part, creates a welcoming atmosphere at Eatery on Main for everyone who walks through the door.

Eatery on Main's Ferrero Rocher Cheesecake

—

> » MAKES 1 (10-INCH)
>   CHEESECAKE
> » TIME: 2 HOURS +
>   25 HOURS TO SET

Crust

¾ cup salted butter

3 cups Oreo cookie crumbs

Filling

5 (each 8 oz/226 g)
   packages of cream
   cheese, softened

2 cups granulated sugar

1 cup hazelnut cocoa spread
   (Eatery on Main uses
   Nutella)

⅓ cup cornstarch

1 Tbsp vanilla extract

2 large eggs

1 cup whipping (35%) cream

10 Ferrero Rocher
   chocolates

Chocolate Ganache
   Topping

2 cups semi-sweet
   chocolate chips

¾ cup whipping (35%)
   cream

12 Ferrero Rocher
   chocolates

This dessert is the ultimate indulgence for chocolate and cheesecake lovers. It has been a customer favourite at Eatery on Main for years, and people order it any time of day—even for breakfast. The middle layer of cheesecake is creamy with a rich chocolatey hazelnut flavour, and the topping is a decadent chocolate ganache, finished with Ferrero Rocher chocolates. It's a recipe that's ideal for a family or holiday gathering, and it absolutely deserves to be savoured alongside a cup of hot coffee, a glass of red wine, or, for something lighter, sparkling lemonade. Note that you have to start this recipe the day before you plan to eat it.

CRUST

1. Preheat the oven to 325°F (165°C). Lightly grease the bottom and sides of a 10-inch springform pan with butter or cooking spray.
2. Place the ¾ cup butter in a medium bowl and place it in the microwave. Heat for 30-second intervals until it is completely melted. Mix in the cookie crumbs until well combined. Pour the mixture into the cheesecake pan and pack the crumbs down on the bottom and 1 inch up the sides to form a crust. Set aside while you prepare the filling.

FILLING

1. Place the cream cheese in a medium bowl and, using a handheld electric mixer, beat it on high speed until light and fluffy. Add the sugar and beat until well combined, scraping down the bottom and sides of the bowl every so often.
2. Add the hazelnut spread, cornstarch, and vanilla and beat again until smooth.
3. Add the eggs one at a time, beating well between additions. Add the cream and beat on low speed until well combined.
4. Chop the Ferrero Rochers into small, medium, and large-sized pieces for variety, and then, using a spatula, gently fold the pieces into the cheesecake filling.
5. Pour the filling on top of the crust in the cheesecake pan and use the spatula to spread it evenly overtop of the crust. Place the cheesecake pan on a rimmed baking sheet. (This ensures there are no leaks and makes it easier to remove from the oven.) Bake the cheesecake on the centre rack of the oven until it is starting to brown around the edges, about 1½ hours. After baking, it should be wiggly in the centre, but not wet.

6. Remove the cheesecake from the oven and let it cool in the pan at room temperature. Once it is cool, cover it tightly with plastic wrap and refrigerate for 24 hours to set.

CHOCOLATE GANACHE TOPPING

1. Once the cheesecake is done setting, place the chocolate chips and whipping cream in a medium bowl and melt them in the microwave for 30-second intervals, stirring between each interval. Watch carefully so that the chocolate does not burn.

TO ASSEMBLE

1. Remove the cheesecake from the fridge. Pour the topping evenly overtop of the filling.
2. Cut 6 of the Ferrero Rochers in half, and place the halves evenly around the perimeter of the cheesecake. Cut the remaining 6 into small, crumbly pieces and sprinkle them overtop of the whole cheesecake.
3. Wrap the finished cheesecake loosely with plastic wrap, being careful not to let it touch the top of the cheesecake, and refrigerate for at least 1 hour to allow the topping to set.
4. Remove the cheesecake from the fridge and carefully remove the sides of the pan. Cut the cheesecake into 12 or 16 slices, and then serve immediately. To prevent the cheesecake from sticking to the knife, you may need to run the knife under warm water prior to cutting.

955C Waskesiu Drive
Waskesiu Lake, SK S0J 2Y0
(306) 663-9534
restaurantpietrowask.wixsite.
com/restaurantpietro
Open from May to
September

RESTAURANT PIETRO

Located in the picturesque resort village of Waskesiu Lake, Restaurant Pietro offers lake-goers the chance to savour the finer things in life. Renowned for its exceptional, streamlined service and first-class food, the restaurant's menu features handmade pasta, fresh seafood, and hand-cut steaks, along with perfect wine pairings, selected by their in-house sommelier.

Co-owners Gary Gagne and Evan Niekamp are both from Saskatoon but have roots in the Waskesiu restaurant scene, which is where they initially met. Gary has a background in fine dining, having worked at the former John's Prime Rib & Steakhouse in Saskatoon and the Fairmont Banff Springs Hotel. He opened the popular Pizza Pete's, now called Pete's Terrace, in Waskesiu in 1989. As a Red Seal chef, Evan brings a wealth of knowledge to the kitchen, having worked at Boffins Public House in Saskatoon and the Waskesiu Golf Course clubhouse restaurant. He's also a trained butcher and he puts his butchering skills into practice at Pietro, preparing specialty cuts of meat in-house for the restaurant.

Restaurant Pietro opened in 2014 and over the years has become a well-loved spot for lake locals and vacationers alike. Gary notes that impeccable customer service has helped to shape their strong reputation, and he's passionate about ensuring customers are treated as guests. The incredible food and service are matched only by the restaurant itself, which has an open kitchen and is timelessly elegant, built of materials like tile, onyx, and chrome. It's this keen attention to detail that gives the restaurant an atmosphere that is uniquely welcoming and polished at the same time. With the charming scenic setting of Waskesiu and Prince Albert National Park as a backdrop, Restaurant Pietro is certainly an ideal spot to soak up a summertime evening. They'll take care of the rest.

Restaurant Pietro's Tableside Caesar Salad

—

> » MAKES 2 APPETIZER SERVINGS
> » TIME: 30 MINUTES
> » GLUTEN-FREE (OPTION)

Croutons

½ fresh baguette, cut into ½-inch cubes (gluten-free if preferred)

⅓ cup olive oil

¾ tsp freshly ground black pepper

Caesar Salad

1 large head of romaine lettuce, washed and dried

3 anchovy fillets

2 garlic cloves, minced

1½ tsp freshly ground black pepper

1½ Tbsp Worcestershire sauce

1 egg yolk

⅓ cup olive oil

¼ cup red wine vinegar

2 Tbsp freshly squeezed lemon juice

½ cup thinly shaved Parmigiano-Reggiano

Gary brought this recipe to Restaurant Pietro after making thousands of Caesar salads during his years in the fine-dining business. This customer favourite is an experience in itself, as it is prepared tableside by Gary, right before your eyes, on his custom salad cart. You can't help but be impressed as you watch him whisk the dressing with the perfect ratio of ingredients, a process he's honed over the years. Whether you're enjoying the full experience at Pietro or trying this at-home version, this light, crisp salad is an ideal way to start a meal.

CROUTONS

1. Preheat the oven to 400°F (200°C) and line a rimmed baking sheet with parchment paper.
2. Place the bread cubes, oil, and pepper in a medium bowl. Mix together thoroughly, ensuring all the bread cubes are evenly coated.
3. Spread the croutons evenly across the prepared baking sheet. Bake until golden brown, 8–10 minutes. Flip them over at the halfway point to ensure they are evenly toasted. Remove them from the oven and set them aside to cool in the pan.

CAESAR SALAD

1. Cut the lettuce leaves into bite-size pieces and place them in a large serving bowl.
2. Place the anchovies, garlic, pepper, and Worcestershire sauce in a medium mixing bowl. Using the back of a fork, mash all the ingredients together until they form a uniform paste.
3. Add the egg yolk, oil, vinegar, and lemon juice to the paste mixture, and mix with a fork or whisk until everything is well combined and has a smooth consistency.
4. Pour the dressing evenly overtop of the prepared lettuce in the bowl. Using salad spoons or tongs, toss the salad lightly until it is evenly coated with the dressing. Add the croutons and toss it again.
5. Separate the salad into portions and garnish with the Parmigiano-Reggiano. Serve immediately.

Restaurant Pietro's Saskatoon Berry Iced Tea

—

» MAKES 16 CUPS
» TIME: 30 MINUTES + 45 MINUTES TO STEEP
» GLUTEN-FREE + VEGAN (OPTION)

16 cups water
4 cups fresh or frozen Saskatoon berries
1½ cups granulated sugar
3 black tea or orange pekoe tea bags*
¼ cup honey or maple syrup (maple syrup for a vegan option)
Ice cubes, for serving
Saskatoon berries, orange slices, fresh mint, or lemon wedges (optional, for garnish)

Saskatoon berry iced tea has been on Restaurant Pietro's menu since it first opened. It is both served on its own and used as a base in many of their signature cocktails. Try incorporating it into a fruity sangria or spiking it by adding a shot of your favourite hard alcohol. You can also reduce or increase the honey or maple syrup in this recipe to adjust the sweetness to your liking. Featuring a Prairie classic, Saskatoon berries, this iced tea offers a distinctly Saskatchewan take on a staple warm weather drink and is the perfect refresher on a hot summer's day.

1. Place the water, Saskatoon berries, and sugar in a large pot. The water should sit at least 3 inches below the top of the pot so that it does not boil over. Cover the pot and bring the mixture to a boil over high heat.
2. Once boiling, turn down the heat to medium-low, remove the lid, and simmer, stirring occasionally, for 15 minutes. The berries will remain whole during this process, but you can crush them lightly with a mixing spoon to extract more of the juice for a stronger flavour, if desired.
3. Add the tea bags to the pot and allow them to steep, still on medium-low heat, for 5 minutes. Stir gently to ensure they are fully submerged in the water.
4. Add the honey, and stir to dissolve completely. Add a bit more honey to taste, if needed.
5. Remove the pot from the heat, and allow it to steep and cool at room temperature, uncovered, until the tea is lukewarm, about 45 minutes. Stir occasionally to ensure it cools evenly.
6. Strain the mixture through a fine-mesh sieve into a large pitcher or jug and discard the berries and tea bags. Serve immediately over ice, or refrigerate to chill prior to serving. Garnish with Saskatoon berries, orange slices, mint, or lemon wedges (if using).

*Both caffeinated and decaffeinated tea work equally well in this recipe.

Tip: For a Saskatoon berry and blueberry iced tea version, use a combination of Saskatoon berries and blueberries at 2 cups each.

Sourcing tip: For where to find Saskatoon berries, see the Sourcing Local Guide (page 291).

Central

—

This chapter has more recipes for baked goods than any of the others, and features many treasured spots in central Saskatchewan's rural communities—some of which have been cherished for decades. In my interviews for this chapter, business owners and bakers alike referenced just how closely food and nostalgia are intertwined within their communities. It's incredible that something as simple as catching a whiff of apple pie as it bakes or sinking your teeth into a certain donut can bring back a flood of fond memories, be it of a specific place or a moment in time.

My own nostalgia around food centres on family traditions and the women in my life. My mom is a home economics teacher, and so from an early age my sister and I were involved in the kitchen. Growing up, we would often make treats like sugar cookies for Halloween, Valentine's Day, or Christmas. The day before we planned to bake, my mom would prepare the cookie dough, mixing and kneading until she'd formed a smooth, supple dough. She'd then portion the dough into several balls, wrapping each one carefully in wax paper before putting them into the fridge to chill. Eating the dough from the fridge was never allowed, but I simply could not resist sneaking a taste. Later in the evening, I'd venture down to the basement fridge, pinch off small pieces of the cool, sugary dough, and pop them into my mouth before scampering back upstairs.

The next day, out would come the large Tupperware bin filled with an assortment of cookie cutters: hearts, snowmen, pumpkins, trees, you name it. As my mom rolled out the dough, my sister and I would cut the cookies and gently place them on the baking sheets. While they baked, she'd mix bowls of buttercream icing with food colouring. We'd spend the afternoon topping the golden cookies with colourful icing and an assortment of candies, delicately placed for eyes on a pumpkin or buttons on a snowman.

For this reason, sugar cookies always remind me of those long afternoons spent decorating, *and eating*, mountains of them with my mom and sister. My dad was always in the background on these afternoons, quietly cleaning up after us girls as we got icing all over the place. In the days that followed, he'd drive us around, visiting family and dropping off plates of our creations. My husband has similar memories about sugar cookies—mainly of eating them—and come the holidays, he still looks forward to receiving an ice-cream pail full of them from his grandma. On occasion, I have tried to recreate these cookies for him, but somehow the icing is always wrong—Grandma's recipe is just one of those things you don't mess with.

Other food items can bring me back to a certain moment just as easily. Mixed candied fruit reminds me of eating my baba's cinnamon buns, which feature little jellies tucked into the dough. Similarly, when I was growing up, my grandma would make three-piece buns for holidays, which brings back happy memories of family gatherings at my grandparents' house, stuffing my face with buns alongside cousins. Recently, I discovered these buns are actually called cloverleaf dinner rolls, but they'll always be Grandma's three-piece buns in my mind.

The food traditions we keep and eateries we go to hold memories, creating meaning through our long-standing attachment to them. Businesses that have stood the test of time—like many in central Saskatchewan—often possess a nostalgic quality for the regulars who frequent them, turning menu staples into much more than meets the eye. At home, nostalgia gives us that same power to link the past with the present, simply through what we can create in the kitchen.

108 Burrows Avenue West
Melfort, SK S0E 1A0
(306) 752-5700
facebook.com/
GoldenGrainBakery

GOLDEN GRAIN BAKERY

Burrows Avenue West in Melfort has been home to bakeries since 1908, when Wood's Bakery and Confectionary opened at 108, and Graham Bakery opened across the street at 101B. Through the years both addresses have housed many bakeries under different names and owners, contributing to over a century of freshly baked goods right in Melfort's downtown.

Today 108 Burrows is home to the beloved Golden Grain Bakery, which was opened by Murray and Mariette McDermid in 1986. The couple were living in Calgary when they received word that Rogers' Family Bakery at 108 was for sale. Murray was a journeyman baker and had always dreamed of opening his own shop, so, after an encouraging visit to Melfort, the couple packed up and moved to Saskatchewan. They named the bakery Golden Grain after their main ingredient and the ripe yellow colour of wheat at harvest.

The McDermids added a coffee shop to the bakery's front, and Murray began offering sweet treats and light lunches of soups and sandwiches on freshly made sub buns. Some popular favourites soon emerged: big foot donuts (they bought a special foot-shaped dough cutter for this signature item), cinnamon buns, and the bismark, an apple and raspberry jam–filled donut topped with icing. The bismark itself has a history that parallels that of Melfort's bakeries, going back to the 1970s and possibly even earlier. The exact date that this tradition started is unclear, but what's certain is its long-standing popularity. Customers specifically make a trip or stop through to pick up donuts, and bismarks and big feet alike have been shipped to Alberta and as far as Toronto.

In 2006, the current owners, Don and Pat Neher, took over Golden Grain. For years prior, Don had been working at a bank across the street and would often wander over to grab lunch and chat with Murray. Coincidentally, Pat taught at the same school where Mariette worked part-time, and the four became close friends. In 1998, Don left his job to apprentice under Murray. Don fondly recalls watching his mom bake when he was growing up and has always liked the idea of starting the day by creating a flawless batch of donuts, bread, or buns.

Many of the bakery's recipes have remained the same over the years, and

the top sellers are still bismarks and big feet, plus their breads and caramel coconut long johns. The key to treasured recipes standing the test of time lies in their being passed down, so when Murray first opened Golden Grain, he hired Trent Rogers, who owned the bakery's previous iteration, Rogers' Family Bakery. Trent handed the bismark recipe and other traditions off to Murray, insisting that community favourites be kept alive. To bring things full circle, Trent now works at Golden Grain, baking full-time with Don.

My husband's mom's side of the family lives in Melfort, so I was first introduced to bismarks on an early visit there when someone picked up a bag of them for coffee time. Having never heard of them before, I accidentally referred to them as "bismacks" and was quickly corrected, but now whenever we visit Melfort a trip to the bakery is a must. For years the outside of 108 Burrows was fittingly painted a bright sunny yellow, and in addition to housing the much-loved bakery, it's also the home of many cherished memories for locals and visitors alike. Golden Grain encapsulates the cozy, familiar feeling of a Prairie bakery, where sweet treats are baked from scratch and nostalgia is always just a freshly made donut away.

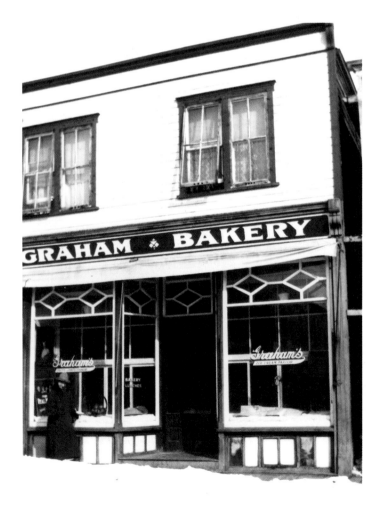

The Graham Bakery was one of the bakeries housed at 108 Burrows Avenue West prior to Golden Grain. It was owned by H. Graham, who initially started the business at 101B Burrows in 1908. He later moved the bakery to 108 Burrows in 1913, and added an ice cream parlour at the back of the building. This photo was taken in the early 1920s.

Golden Grain Bakery's Bismarks with Buttercream Icing or Danish Roll Icing

—

» MAKES 12 BISMARKS
» TIME: 1½ HOURS +
   1½ HOURS TO RISE

Bismarks

2¾ cups bread flour or all-purpose flour, divided

3 Tbsp granulated sugar

1 (2¼ tsp) packet instant yeast

½ tsp fine salt

1 cup whole milk, warmed to 40–46°C (105–115°F)*

3 large egg yolks

1½ tsp vanilla extract

¼ cup unsalted butter, at room temperature

⅓ cup apple-raspberry jam**

Vegetable oil, for deep frying

Buttercream Icing

1 cup salted butter, at room temperature

4 cups icing sugar

4–5 Tbsp coffee cream (18% or higher)

3 tsp vanilla extract

Danish Roll Icing

4 cups icing sugar

4–8 Tbsp water

½ tsp vanilla extract

Bismarks are a yeast donut, filled with gooey jam and topped with sugary sweet icing, making them a perfect indulgence to pair with a steaming cup of coffee. Golden Grain offers chocolate, iced, and glazed bismarks, all made fresh daily. This recipe features two icing options: buttercream icing, which is the traditional bismark topping used by Melfort bakeries for years, and Danish roll icing, which Murray started using for bismarks in the late 1980s. Customers who grew up with a certain icing gracing their bismarks will tell you *that icing* is best—but I'll let you be the judge.

BISMARKS

1. In the bowl of a stand mixer fitted with the dough hook, mix together 2 cups of the flour, the sugar, yeast, and salt on low speed until combined. With the mixer still running on low speed, slowly add the warm milk, egg yolks, and vanilla. Increase the speed to medium and mix until smooth.

2. Add the remaining ¾ cup of flour and the butter. Mix again on medium speed until the dough is soft, smooth, and slightly sticky.

3. Cover the bowl tightly with plastic wrap and set it in a draft-free place to rise until doubled in size, about 1 hour. (Alternatively, you can refrigerate it for up to 12 hours and it will rise in the fridge. If you choose this option, remove from the fridge to sit at room temperature for 15 minutes before using.)

4. Lightly dust flour onto two rimmed baking sheets and a clean countertop.

5. Using a rolling pin, roll out the dough on the countertop until it is about ¼-inch thick.

6. Using a floured 3-inch non-tapered cookie cutter (or 3-inch diameter water glass), cut the dough into 12 circles. Place 6 circles of dough on each prepared baking sheet. Space them apart evenly. If you have any dough scraps, set them aside to fry later for smaller donut pieces.

7. Place about 1 tsp of the apple-raspberry jam into the centre of each dough circle for the filling.

8. Using a pastry brush dipped in water, moisten the outer edge of the bottom half of each circle. Fold the top half of each circle up to meet the bottom edge, pressing firmly around the edges with your fingertips to seal the dough. The end result should look like a perogy. The completed bismarks should be at least 1 inch apart.

9. Cover them loosely with plastic wrap and set in a warm place to rise until they are puffy and nearly double in size, about

30 minutes. To check if they are ready, touch them gently with your fingertip. The dough should spring back slowly. If it springs back immediately, they need a bit more rising time.

10. When the bismarks are about halfway through their second rise, fill a large, heavy-bottomed pot with at least 2 inches of vegetable oil. The oil should not come up more than halfway along the side of the pot. Heat the oil over medium-high heat until an instant-read thermometer reads 360°F (180°C). (Alternatively, if you have a deep fryer you can use that to fry the bismarks. Follow the instructions for your brand of deep fryer.)

11. Once the bismarks have completed their second rise, use a spatula or slotted spoon to carefully lower them in batches of 2 to 4 into the hot oil. Be careful not to overcrowd the pot; otherwise, they will not fry properly. Fry each bismark, turning once or twice, until they are a light golden brown colour and cooked through, 1–2 minutes per side. Carefully remove the fried bismarks from the oil with a slotted spoon and let them cool and drain on a wire cooling rack, set over several layers of paper towel.

12. Repeat with the remaining bismarks and any dough scraps, ensuring the temperature is consistent at 360°F (180°C). You may need to let the oil come back to temperature between batches. Let all the bismarks cool completely at room temperature.

13. Prepare your icing of choice while the bismarks are cooling (below).

14. Leftover bismarks can be kept in an airtight container in a cool place for 2–3 days, but not in the fridge, as they will stale quickly if refrigerated. (Alternatively, uniced bismarks can be packaged in plastic bags, with as much of the air removed as possible, and stored in the freezer for up to 1 month. When ready to use, thaw the bismarks at room temperature and then ice them.)

BUTTERCREAM ICING

1. Place the butter in a large bowl. Using a handheld electric mixer on low speed, begin to beat the butter. Gradually increase the speed to medium, until the butter is light and creamy.

2. Add the icing sugar and beat until well combined.

3. Add 4 Tbsp of the coffee cream and the vanilla, and beat again until smooth. For stiffer icing, use less cream, and for lighter icing, use more.

4. Use a butter knife or an offset spatula to apply the icing to the bismarks. Leftover icing can be stored in an airtight container in the freezer for up to 2 months. Thaw it in the fridge and rewhip with an electric mixer prior to using.

DANISH ROLL ICING

1. Whisk together all of the ingredients in a medium mixing bowl until smooth. Start by adding 4 Tbsp of water, and add up to a maximum of 8 Tbsp to achieve the desired consistency. The icing should be thick enough that it does not run off the bismarks.

2. Use a butter knife or an offset spatula to apply the icing to the bismarks. Leftover icing can be stored in an airtight container in the freezer for up to 2 months. Thaw it in the fridge and rewhip by hand or with a mixer prior to using, adding water or icing sugar as needed to reach the desired consistency.

*To warm the milk, microwave it in a bowl for about 45 seconds and then check the temperature with an instant-read thermometer. The milk needs to reach a certain temperature in order to activate the yeast.

**Golden Grain uses an apple-raspberry jam for their bismark filling, but raspberry jam can be substituted.

Tip: You only need one batch of icing for the bismarks—but you could make both icings and use half of each, storing the rest for another baking day.

701 Railway Avenue
Rosthern, SK S0K 3R0
(306) 232-5332
stationarts.com

STATION ARTS CENTRE

Housed in a historic Canadian National Railway station, the Station Arts Centre is a fixture in Rosthern, bringing history, culture, arts, and great food together under one roof. The restaurant portion, known for years as the Tea Room, has been an integral part of the organization since its beginning, providing light lunches and sweet treats to visitors, and hosting dinners in conjunction with live events at their in-house theatre.

With over a century of history, the station is one of just two like it in the province. Constructed in 1902, it was viewed as a symbol of growth, providing transportation for both people and goods to and from the Rosthern area. The main floor of the building initially held an office and large waiting room, while the second floor housed the station agent's living quarters. For years it was a bustling stop that saw countless travellers, and, as a result, the Station Arts Centre often welcomes visitors today who are looking for historical clues to their family roots.

In 1981, the train service was discontinued. The building was designated a Municipal Heritage Property in 1982, but it began to deteriorate through lack of use. In the mid-1980s, a group of Rosthern residents had the idea of turning the station into an arts centre to save and make use of the building. They created the Station Arts Centre Co-Operative and began hosting events in town to raise money and awareness. The Town of Rosthern agreed to lease the building for the creation of an arts and cultural hub, and in 1989 the Station Arts Centre officially opened its doors.

The Station has undergone renovations since, but many original heritage details have been preserved, giving it historic charm. The dining area weaves throughout the main floor, offering the experience of dining in a gallery. The space is bright and airy, with natural light streaming in through picture windows that overlook the train platforms.

For over three decades, the restaurant portion of the Station operated as the Tea Room, which offered a lunch and dessert menu with made-from-scratch favourites like homemade bread and fresh soups. It was managed by different people throughout the years, including siblings Dennis Helmuth and Joan Yoder, and Robert Schellenberg. In 2021, their retirement brought an end to the Tea

63

Room era, but the Station has plans to continue offering food in the future. Coffee, craft beer, desserts, and pop-up restaurant events are in the works, so that guests can continue to enjoy locally sourced food and drink when they visit.

Today, the Station Arts Centre is a recognized Arts Council with the Organization of Saskatchewan Arts Councils and is very much the artistic hub it was intended to be, hosting art exhibits, workshops, and live music and theatre. Part of what makes the Station Arts Centre so special is that it provides both a gathering space and an outlet for artistic expression, thanks to the efforts of an extensive network of volunteers who make it all happen. It's also a source of nostalgia for many, including Josie LaChance, director of operations, and Nicole Thiessen, director of programming, who both grew up in the area. Josie fondly remembers visiting the station for lunch and Christmas events, and Nicole's mom, Kathy Thiessen, was one of the founders in the 1980s. Both agree that their ultimate goal is to create positive change through art and culture by bridging big-city experiences with small-town charm. One thing's clear: whether you come for the food or the show, the Station Arts Centre is a gem on the Prairies, providing a rare mix of culinary, artistic, and historical experiences in rural Saskatchewan.

This postcard shows a side view of the Rosthern Train Station in 1909, with railcars on the right side. The note on the postcard reads: "Leaving for Manitoba Nov. 3 – 1909. Taken by B.B. Louven."

The Tea Room's Cheddar Tomato Quiche

—

» MAKES 1 (9-INCH) QUICHE
» TIME: 1 HOUR 30 MINUTES

Crust

¾ cup all-purpose flour

½ cup cornmeal

¼ tsp sea salt

¼ tsp ground black pepper

⅓ cup salted butter, cold and cubed

¼ cup cold water

Filling

2 cups medium-diced Roma tomatoes

4 scallions, diced small, or ½ cup small-diced yellow onion

1 tsp salt

½ tsp granulated sugar

½ tsp dried basil

¼ tsp ground black pepper

1 cup shredded old cheddar cheese*

3 large eggs

1 cup evaporated milk

2 Tbsp all-purpose flour

This quiche was a Tea Room favourite that regularly appeared on their feature menu, showcasing ripe red Roma tomatoes sourced locally in season. The quiche has a savoury tomato basil flavour, and the addition of cornmeal to the crust adds a distinctly light and flaky touch. This recipe is from former Tea Room manager Dennis Helmuth, who operated the restaurant with his sister Joan Yoder for 26 years. It's a family favourite that they've adapted over the years. Serve this as the main event for brunch or lunch, alongside soup, a green salad, or fresh fruit.

CRUST

1. Preheat the oven to 375°F (190°C). Lightly grease a 9-inch pie pan with cooking spray.
2. Place the flour, cornmeal, salt, and pepper in a medium mixing bowl. Stir to combine.
3. Add the butter to the bowl and, using a pastry cutter, cut it into the flour mixture until it becomes crumbly and is well combined and you can see pea-sized pieces of butter. Sprinkle the cold water overtop of the mixture, while tossing with a fork. Stir lightly until the mixture forms a ball.
4. Lightly flour a clean surface. Using a rolling pin, roll out the dough until it is ⅛-inch thick and then fit it loosely into the greased pie pan, gently pressing it down. Trim the edges with a knife, fold them over, or flute them.
5. Bake the crust for 10 minutes, and then remove it from the oven and set it aside while you prepare the filling. Keep the oven on.

FILLING

1. Spread the tomatoes evenly around the baked crust.
2. Place the scallions, salt, sugar, basil, and pepper in a small bowl. Stir them all together and then sprinkle the mixture overtop of the tomatoes. Sprinkle the shredded cheese evenly overtop of everything.
3. Place the eggs, evaporated milk, and flour in a small bowl and, using a fork, whisk them together until there are no lumps. Pour this mixture overtop of the grated cheese.
4. Bake the quiche on the centre rack of the oven, until the filling is set and the crust is golden brown, 40–45 minutes.

5. Remove the quiche from the oven and let cool for 5 minutes before cutting. Serve immediately.

*A combination of your favourite cheeses can be used for this recipe, to equal 1 cup shredded cheese.

Tip: You can prepare the crust and place it in the pie pan in advance and refrigerate, covered with plastic wrap, for up to 1 day prior to baking.

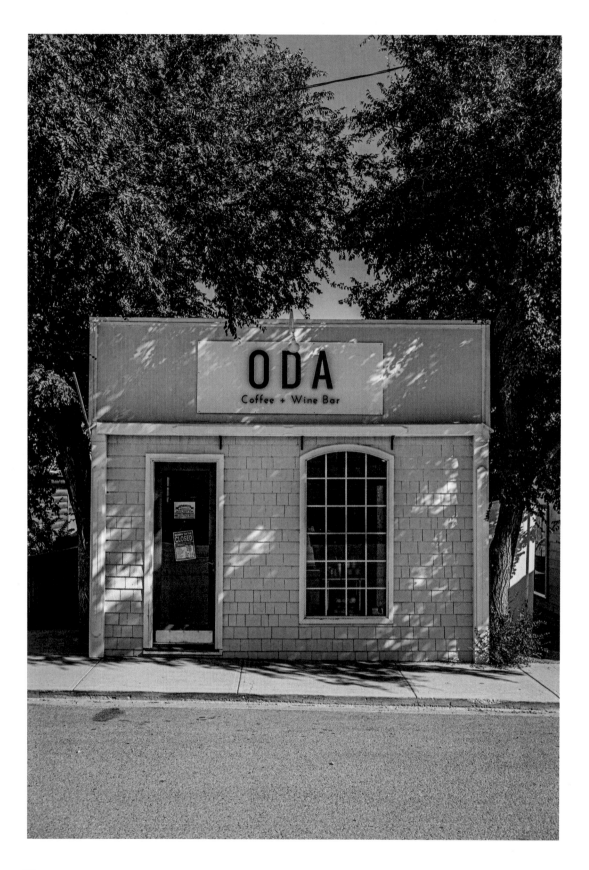

305 MacLachlan Avenue
Manitou Beach, SK S0K 4T1
(306) 952-5493
facebook.com/
Odacoffeeandwine
Open from May to
September

ODA COFFEE + WINE BAR

Along the shores of Little Manitou Lake sits Manitou Beach, an adorable resort village that is home to restaurants, shops, and a mineral spa. Come summertime, Manitou is always bustling with tourists and locals alike, all eager to take a dip in the lake's legendary salt waters.

Right on the beach is Oda Coffee + Wine Bar, a charming little café that is fittingly painted a bright seafoam blue. Owner Lane Manson is originally from Watrous and has owned and operated the Manitou Hotel and Bar for years. He bought the café with his sister in 2018 and introduced not only an extensive wine and cocktail menu, but also a private supper dining service that offers guests curated multicourse menus. In addition, Lane hosts events alongside local happenings, like wine tastings and a champagne and snack service during Manitou's annual fireworks.

When you walk into Oda, a long corridor leads you to the back room, where big picture windows look right onto the water and fill the café with soft natural light. Vintage tables and ornate chandeliers add colour to the space, while local art lines the walls, a nod to Manitou's thriving art community. A large wraparound deck right on the beach offers stunning lake views, making it an ideal setting to enjoy brunch, lunch, or one of Oda's homemade desserts, along with a summertime cocktail.

Manitou Beach is also home to many attractions worth a visit, like the iconic Danceland Ballroom, which was constructed in 1928 and boasts a dance floor built on horsehair to cushion dancers' feet. The lake is an attraction in itself, of course, and is commonly referred to as the Dead Sea of Canada, due to the water's high salt and mineral content, which means you can float. Be sure to snap a photo of yourself while you're lying back in the water, book in hand—it's a Manitou must.

Oda's Rhubarb Crumble Cake

—

» MAKES 1 (9- × 13-INCH) CAKE
» TIME: 1 HOUR 30 MINUTES

Cake Topping
½ cup all-purpose flour
½ cup packed brown sugar
¼ cup salted butter, softened
1 tsp ground cinnamon

Rhubarb Crumble Cake
1 cup packed brown sugar
½ cup salted butter, softened
1 large egg
1 tsp vanilla extract
2 cups all-purpose flour
1 tsp baking soda
¼ tsp sea salt
1 cup 1% or 2% milk
2 cups fresh or frozen
    chopped (1-inch pieces)
    rhubarb

Optional Garnish
Vanilla ice cream or
    whipped cream,
    for serving
Ground cinnamon

As a perennial that does well in cold weather, rhubarb is a Saskatchewan garden staple. The first stalks of the spring usually signal one thing: time for baking! This recipe is the perfect excuse to use up fresh new rhubarb or frozen rhubarb from last season. Oda sources their rhubarb locally for this dessert, which is a customer favourite. The cake is moist and fluffy, while the topping provides a satisfying crunch of delicious brown sugar and cinnamon. For best results, pair this with strong coffee or tart lemonade—on a lazy afternoon, of course.

CAKE TOPPING

1. Place the flour, sugar, butter, and cinnamon in a medium bowl. Using a handheld electric mixer, beat on low speed until fine crumbs form, 1–2 minutes. Set the topping aside while you prepare the cake.

RHUBARB CRUMBLE CAKE

1. Preheat the oven to 350°F (180°C). Grease a 9- × 13-inch baking pan with butter or cooking spray, and then lightly flour the bottom and sides of the pan, shaking gently to coat it.
2. Place the sugar and butter in a medium bowl. Using a handheld electric mixer, beat the sugar and butter on medium speed until light and fluffy. Add the egg and vanilla, and beat again until well combined.
3. Place the flour, baking soda, and salt in a small bowl and stir together to combine.
4. Add half the flour mixture and half the milk to the sugar and butter bowl, cream on low speed, and then scrape down the sides of the bowl. Add the remaining flour mixture and milk, and cream again on low speed until the cake batter is smooth, 1–2 minutes.
5. Using a spatula, gently fold the rhubarb into the batter until fully incorporated.
6. Transfer the batter to the prepared baking pan and, using a spatula, spread it around the pan evenly. Sprinkle the prepared topping evenly overtop of the cake batter.
7. Bake the cake on the centre rack of the oven until a cake tester inserted into the centre of the cake comes out clean, 45–50 minutes.
8. Remove the cake from the oven and let it cool in the pan for 10–15 minutes. Cut the cake into 12 pieces, and serve immediately with a scoop of vanilla ice cream or whipped cream, and a sprinkle of cinnamon on top (if using).

WADENA BAKERY & COFFEE NOOK

70 Main Street North
Wadena, SK S0A 4J0
(306) 338-2212
wadenabakery.com

Wadena Bakery & Coffee Nook, owned by the Suik family since 1959, is one of the oldest family-run bakeries in the province. Currently operated by Steve and Margaret Suik, who are the second generation of the family to run the business, Wadena Bakery is a popular spot, known for their extensive pastry and donut selection, particularly their legendary Boston creams.

Steve's parents, Leo and Joan Suik, immigrated to Canada in 1954 from the Netherlands and initially settled in Regina. Having trained and worked as a baker for years, Leo began working at the former McGavin's Bakery in Regina. Shortly after, a bakery in Delisle came up for rent, and the couple packed up and moved to Delisle to run it. They wanted to own their own business, however, so when the Wadena Bakery and Tea Room—as it was originally called—came up for sale a few years later, they decided to move again.

In the early days, Wadena Bakery's bestsellers were bread and buns. Over time, the menu expanded to include lunch fare and sweets like pastries, donuts, squares, and pies. Wadena Bakery was also one of the first in the province to offer photo cakes, a rarity at the time.

Steve worked in the bakery from an early age and remembers coming by after school to help his parents out. He would stand on a big lard pail and stamp out tart shells as he watched his dad bake. As a teenager, he began working at the bakery on weekends and summer holidays, learning the ropes and helping to run the daily operations. Margaret also grew up in the Wadena area, and after high school, they both moved to Saskatoon, where they got married. One day they got a call from Leo and Joan, asking if they were interested in buying the family bakery at some point. In 1977, they moved back to Wadena and began working at the bakery full-time, until they officially took over the business in 1987. All five of their kids grew up working at the bakery too, and Leo even came back after retiring to work part-time—forever a baker at heart.

The original Wadena Bakery and Tea Room had a bakery on one side and a tea room on the other, which Leo removed in the 1960s. When Steve and Margaret moved back, they decided to recreate the tea room with the bakery's Coffee Nook, which offers hot and cold beverages as the perfect accompaniment to their freshly baked goods. Their main sellers these days are pastries and donuts, most notably their Boston creams, which come in chocolate, mocha, and salted caramel flavours. In recent years, the Boston creams have gained a solid following, which continues to grow steadily, and Steve estimates that about two-thirds of their daily production is now Boston creams alone. The bakery has become a bit of a tourist attraction, drawing many customers to the area who stop by just to pick up a box of these delicious treats. Of course, the recipe is a well-kept secret, but I assure you, the cool, fluffy cream surrounded by melt-in-your-mouth deep-fried dough really is the stuff of dreams.

As one of just a handful of bakeries like it left in the province, Wadena Bakery is very much a living link to a bygone era when family-owned bakeries dotted the Prairie landscape. Right on Wadena's Main Street, it has that homey, comfortable feeling of a small-town Saskatchewan bakery, and with a history of over 60 years and counting, it has certainly cemented itself as a provincial favourite.

Wadena Bakery's Ollie Bollen

—

» MAKES 24-30 DONUTS
» TIME: 1 HOUR 15 MINUTES
+ 45 MINUTES TO RISE

¼ cup + 1 tsp granulated
   sugar, divided
1½ Tbsp active dry yeast
¼ cup lukewarm water
4¼ cups all-purpose flour
1 tsp sea salt
2 large eggs
2 cups lukewarm 1% or
   2% milk
1 large Granny Smith apple,
   peeled and cut into
   ¼-inch dice
2 cups dark or golden raisins
Vegetable oil, for deep
   frying
Icing sugar, for dusting*

Ollie bollen are a traditional Dutch beignet typically made for the holidays. This recipe is a Suik family favourite, and every December, Leo would fry up a big batch of ollie bollen at Wadena Bakery. Some would go into the bakery's showcase, and the others would go home for New Year's. Steve fondly recalls sitting around the table with family during the holidays, drinking coffee and dunking fresh ollie bollen in a bowl of icing sugar. Ollie bollen are a less sweet donut, so you can increase the level of sweetness by dusting or dunking them in icing sugar—or you can enjoy them plain.

1. Preheat your oven to its lowest setting. Once it reaches temperature, turn it off.
2. Place the 1 tsp of sugar and the yeast in a small bowl with the water. Stir gently with a fork until the sugar and yeast are fully dissolved, and then set aside for 10 minutes to activate.
3. In the bowl of a stand mixer fitted with the paddle attachment, place the remaining ¼ cup of sugar, the flour, and salt. Mix on the lowest speed until well combined.
4. Add the prepared yeast mixture, the eggs, and milk. Mix on medium speed until the dough is smooth and similar to a heavy batter, about 4 minutes.
5. Add the apples and raisins, and mix again gently on low speed, just until they are fully incorporated.
6. Remove the bowl from the stand mixer and place a clean, damp tea towel on top of it. Place the bowl in the warm oven and allow the dough to rise until it has doubled in size, about 45 minutes.
7. If you're using a deep fryer: As soon as you set the dough to rise, preheat your deep fryer to 365°F (185°C). Follow the instructions for your brand of deep fryer.
8. If you're not using a deep fryer, once the dough is almost done rising, fill a large heavy-bottomed pot with at least 3 inches of oil. The oil should not come up more than halfway along the side of the pot, but it should be deep enough for the donuts to float. Heat the oil over medium-high heat until an instant-read thermometer reads 365°F (185°C).
9. Spray the inside of a trigger ice-cream scoop (#20 works well) with cooking spray and carefully drop a scoopful of dough into the hot oil. This is your test ollie. Fry until golden brown, turning once, about 2 minutes on each side. Remove from the oil and place on a rimmed baking sheet lined with paper towel. (If you are frying them in a pot on the stove, use a slotted spoon to carefully remove them from the oil, away from your body.) Check the test

donut to ensure it has cooked properly. If not, fry for a little bit longer until cooked through.

10. Repeat the frying process with the remaining dough. You may need to spray the ice-cream scoop with cooking spray after every few batches so the dough does not stick. If you're using a pot on the stove, ensure the temperature of the oil is consistently 365°F (185°C). The number of donuts you can fry at one time depends on the size of your pot or deep fryer, but be careful not to overcrowd them to ensure they cook properly. Place the completed ones on the rimmed baking sheet to cool at room temperature.

11. Dust the fried ollie bollen with icing sugar to taste, or dunk them in icing sugar for a sweeter flavour. Serve immediately.

12. Leftover ollie bollen can be stored in an airtight container in the freezer, without their sugar coating, for up to 2 months. When you're ready to serve, thaw them at room temperature or warm them up in a microwave oven, and then dust with icing sugar.

*Icing sugar is the traditional topping for ollie bollen, but you can also try dusting or dipping them in cinnamon sugar or granulated sugar.

103 1st Avenue North
Stenen, SK S0A 3X0
(306) 548-2009
rawhides.ca

RAWHIDES BISTRO AND SALOON

Located in the village of Stenen, Rawhides is a popular destination that draws visitors year-round from all across the province. Home to a western-themed restaurant and patio, expansive event centre, and on-site campground, Rawhides offers an atmosphere and experience unlike any other.

Co-owners Doug Will and his son, Frazer Will, have a background in agriculture and farming, and operate an alfalfa mill in nearby Norquay. When Doug and his late wife, Brenda, opened Rawhides, they wanted to replace the King George Hotel, which had burned down in 2011. The hotel had been a fixture in Stenen for over a century, and the fire left the surrounding communities with nowhere to gather. The couple purchased Stenen's old four-room schoolhouse, which had closed in 1987, with the intention of repurposing the building into a restaurant. Construction began in May of 2012, and Doug and Brenda designed everything themselves, with practical input from local con-tractors. Rawhides opened on the August long weekend of that same year, just in time for Stenen's 100th anniversary celebration.

The schoolhouse's long hallway runs through the restaurant's centre, with the former classrooms branching off from the hall. Each classroom has been turned into a themed room in the restaurant, such as the Library, which features shelves of old books from the schoolhouse. The space is decorated with antique and rustic features like lanterns, saddles, and barbwire, and the schoolhouse's original brick can be seen prominently throughout, painted different colours in each room. The office where the Rawhides' staff works is the former principal's office, a detail remembered by many customers who attended the school. Doug notes that one particular customer even shared a story about how he ended up in the principal's office for drinking outside the school—ironically, there he was 50 years later, enjoying a beer in that same spot.

Rawhides' large event centre was added in 2015 and, in keeping with the western theme, was designed to resemble a horse barn. The event centre is constructed of wood and features a loft, which creates a stunning grand interior, while wagon wheel chandeliers hang overhead, filling the space with soft light when the sun goes down. Double doors lead outside onto the patio, where picnic tables and fire pits provide a country setting. It's a popular location for weddings and anniversary celebrations, and there is a variety of entertainment like live music in summertime. The western theme extends beyond the décor to the menu, which features barbeque favourites like steak, burgers, and ribs, as well as newer additions like pizza and pasta.

Prior to visiting, I had heard about just how genuinely cool Rawhides is, but I have to say that photos simply don't do it justice—it's something you have to see for yourself. Rooted in history and bursting with eccentric character, Rawhides feels incredibly Saskatchewan, from the décor and the food to the visitors who drive for hours just to enjoy a meal there. Given that the population of Stenen clocks in at under 100 people, Doug notes that Rawhides has become a "community of communities." He estimates that over the years they've had close to a million customers from every corner of the province. It goes without saying that when the place is packed, it vibrates with energy, truly serving as the community spot it was always intended to be.

The King George Hotel was a staple gathering place in Stenen for over a century, until it burned down in 2011. Doug and Brenda Will opened Rawhides to provide a new community space for Stenen and the surrounding area.

Rawhides' Smokehouse Baby Back Ribs and BBQ Sauce

—

» MAKES 6-8 SERVINGS
» TIME: 3-4 HOURS
» GLUTEN-FREE (OPTION)

Dry Seasoning

2 Tbsp smoked paprika

2 Tbsp granulated onion powder

2 Tbsp dried oregano

2 Tbsp kosher salt or sea salt

2 Tbsp brown sugar

2 Tbsp cracked black peppercorns

¼ tsp chili powder

Smokehouse Baby Back Ribs

6 (about 1½ lb per rib) baby back pork ribs

Fresh or fried chopped green onions (optional)

Smokehouse BBQ Sauce

2 tsp butter or margarine

2 garlic cloves, minced

2 small shallots, diced small

2 Tbsp store-bought BBQ sauce (gluten-free if preferred)

2 tsp smoked paprika

1 tsp brown sugar

1 tsp kosher salt or sea salt

1 tsp ground black pepper

1 cup ketchup

2 Tbsp pineapple juice

2 tsp dark soy sauce* (gluten-free if preferred)

1 tsp apple cider vinegar

½ tsp liquid smoke**

Smokehouse baby back ribs, slow-cooked and glazed in a deliciously sweet, smokey BBQ sauce, have been a popular item on Rawhides' menu from the very beginning. This recipe is from their head chef, Isagani Puyos. Isagani is originally from the Philippines and started at Rawhides in 2013 as a line cook, before becoming head chef in 2015. His wife, Alma, is Rawhides' sous chef. The couple spent years working in the Philippines and Cayman Islands before moving to Canada. This recipe is perfect for a summertime barbeque, and pairs well with coleslaw, french fries, or baked potatoes.

DRY SEASONING AND SMOKEHOUSE BABY BACK RIBS

1. Preheat the grill or barbeque to 375°F (190°C) and preheat the oven to 275°F (135°C). If available, use the convection setting on your oven.
2. Place all the seasoning ingredients in a small bowl, and stir together to combine.
3. Put the ribs on rimmed baking sheets and lightly rub them with the seasoning, ensuring they are evenly covered on both sides.
4. Grill the ribs on both sides to create light grill marks, 3-4 minutes per side. They should be lightly golden brown after this point. Watch carefully so that they do not burn.
5. Pour 1 cup of water into a roasting pan large enough to hold the ribs without crowding and then add the grilled ribs. Cover the pan tightly with aluminum foil or a lid. Cook the ribs in the oven for 1 hour. After 1 hour, turn down the oven temperature to 200°F (93°C) and continue to cook the ribs until the meat is cooked through and pulls apart easily from the bones, 1½ to 2½ hours. The total cooking time will depend on your oven and whether or not the convection setting is used.
6. While they cook, prepare the BBQ sauce (below).
7. Remove the ribs from the oven and, using tongs, transfer them to a rimmed baking sheet. (You may need more than one baking sheet.) Turn the oven temperature up to 350°F (180°C). Using a silicone barbeque brush, spread the prepared BBQ sauce evenly on both sides of the ribs. Put the ribs back in the oven to create a warm glaze with the sauce, 2-5 minutes.
8. Remove the ribs from the oven and top with the green onions (if using). Serve immediately, either as a whole rack or cut into individual ribs.

SMOKEHOUSE BBQ SAUCE

1. Place the butter in a medium saucepan and melt it over medium heat. Add the garlic and shallots, and cook until lightly browned and translucent, about 5 minutes.
2. Add the remaining sauce ingredients and stir to combine. Heat the sauce over low heat, uncovered, until it reaches a light simmer, about 5 minutes. Stir regularly to ensure it does not burn. After about 5 minutes, it should have a thick BBQ sauce-like consistency.
3. Remove the sauce from the heat and let it settle and cool slightly at room temperature prior to glazing the ribs. If you make the sauce ahead of time, you can let it cool completely at room temperature and then refrigerate it in an airtight container for up to 1 week.

*Dark soy sauce is darker and thicker than regular soy sauce but not salty. Look for it in the international section of the grocery store or at an Asian grocery store. If you cannot find gluten-free dark soy sauce, you can substitute it with gluten-free regular soy sauce.

**Look for liquid smoke in the spice, baking, or condiment section at the grocery store. You can also find flavoured or specialty brands of liquid smoke at most butcher and deli shops.

SE 36-30-08 W3,
Rudy No. 284
Near Outlook, SK S0L 2N0
(306) 867-9463
wolfwillowwinery.ca
Open from May to
September

WOLF WILLOW WINERY

Wolf Willow Winery is a spectacular destination, home to an organic orchard, winery, restaurant, and glamp ground, all situated along the banks of the South Saskatchewan River. The Vander Schaaf family was initially drawn to the site because of its picturesque landscape, but when they purchased the property, the orchard came with it. Wanting to make use of the fruit, they decided to add a restaurant and winery in 2013. Since then, brothers Joel and Jesse Vander Schaaf have embraced the world of fruit wine and are passionate about its possibilities, noting that it has a boldly sweet and tart flavour profile distinct from grape wine's. Wolf Willow's wines all feature quintessentially Saskatchewan flavours—cherry, rhubarb, and honeyberry (also known as haskap), for example—and the winery also has a canned cocktail line, including delicious summer drinks like Prairie Sangria and Sour Cherry Cola.

In 2017 the family added a glamp ground to the site: Camp Wolf Willow.

The glamp ground has both solar-powered glamping sites and classic tenting sites, and it is surrounded by endless Prairie landscape to explore. The river's beachfront is just a short walk away, and there are hiking and biking trails nearby too, all complete with magnificent views of the South Saskatchewan River valley.

Their on-site restaurant ties it all together with a menu built around camping and outdoor comfort food, like charcuterie, roasted nuts, and handmade pizza. The restaurant's sprawling wood patio overlooks the river valley, and if you visit for dinner, you're almost guaranteed to witness a stunning sunset. Wolf Willow is an ideal destination to spend a weekend, a place where you can slow down and savour a laid-back meal alongside a glass of locally made wine. And the best part? Post-dinner, your luxury tent is just a short stroll away. It doesn't get much better than that.

Wolf Willow's Rosemary Rhubarb Press

—

» MAKES 1 COCKTAIL +
1¼ CUPS SYRUP
» TIME: 30 MINUTES +
30 MINUTES TO STEEP
» GLUTEN-FREE + VEGAN

Rosemary Syrup

1 cup granulated sugar

1 cup water

¼ cup fresh rosemary leaves

Rosemary Rhubarb Press

3 oz Wolf Willow Rhubarb
Wine

1½ Tbsp rosemary syrup
(above)

1½ tsp freshly squeezed
lemon juice

Ice cubes

¼ cup sparkling water

1 lemon wheel, for garnish

1 sprig of fresh rosemary, for
garnish

The rosemary rhubarb press is a light, refreshing cocktail that combines Wolf Willow's Rhubarb Wine with bright citrus and savoury rosemary. This cocktail screams patio vibes with its light pink and peach colour, and pairs well with spicy or salty dishes. The rhubarb wine itself features a Prairie garden staple, rhubarb, which Wolf Willow macerates for a minimum of two weeks to extract the maximum flavour. With a boldly tart and subtly sweet flavour profile, the rhubarb wine also works well in sangrias, spritzers, or chilled on its own.

ROSEMARY SYRUP

1. Place the sugar, water, and rosemary leaves in a small saucepan over medium-high heat. Bring to a boil, uncovered, stirring occasionally, until the sugar dissolves.
2. Once boiling, turn the heat to low and let the mixture simmer, undisturbed, for 1 minute.
3. Remove from the heat and let the syrup steep, uncovered, for 30 minutes.
4. Strain the syrup over a fine-mesh strainer into a glass jar or bowl and discard the rosemary leaves. Let the syrup cool completely and then transfer it to an airtight container.
5. Leftover syrup can be refrigerated in an airtight container for up to 1 month. If it hardens while being stored, simply heat it up for 30 seconds or so in a microwave oven prior to using.

ROSEMARY RHUBARB PRESS

1. Place the wine, syrup, and lemon juice in a cocktail shaker with a few ice cubes. Shake hard for 20 seconds and then strain into a cocktail glass.
2. Add the sparkling water and 2–3 ice cubes, then garnish with a lemon wheel and rosemary sprig, and serve immediately.

Sourcing tip: For where to find Wolf Willow products, see the Sourcing Local Guide (page 292).

Wolf Willow's Smokey Stovetop Popcorn

—

>> MAKES 2 SNACK SERVINGS
>> TIME: 15 MINUTES
>> GLUTEN-FREE + VEGAN

Smokey Topping
¼ cup extra-virgin olive oil
1 Tbsp liquid smoke*

Smokey Stovetop Popcorn
½ cup unpopped popcorn
   kernels
2 Tbsp extra-virgin olive oil
Himalayan rock salt or sea
   salt

This popcorn is a popular item from Wolf Willow's snack menu, created with the classic Jiffy Pop camping experience in mind. Popcorn and camping go hand in hand, and this recipe certainly brings up memories for me of a summertime evening well spent around a campfire. Making popcorn on the stove is easy and gives the popcorn a little bit of extra crunch from being popped directly in oil. You can reduce or increase the smokey flavour of this recipe by adjusting the amount of smokey topping you drizzle on, or by adding smoked or flavoured sea salts, like hickory or mesquite.

SMOKEY TOPPING

1. Mix together the oil and liquid smoke in a small bowl or jar. Set it aside.

SMOKEY STOVETOP POPCORN

1. Place the popcorn kernels and oil in a large pot over medium heat. Cover the pot with its lid and then shake lightly to distribute the oil evenly over the kernels. As the oil heats up, occasionally shake the pot back and forth lightly to ensure even distribution of heat. (You may need to wear oven mitts while shaking.) The popcorn should begin to pop after about 5 minutes. Once the popping slows noticeably, remove the pot from the heat.
2. Transfer the popped popcorn to a large bowl and drizzle the smokey topping overtop. Toss to coat evenly and add some salt. Adjust the seasonings to taste. Serve immediately.

*Look for liquid smoke in the spice, baking, or condiment section at the grocery store. You can also find flavoured or specialty brands of liquid smoke at most butcher and deli shops.

GRAIN & PULSE BAKERY CAFÉ

207 Royal Street
Imperial, SK S0G 2J0
(306) 963-3287
On Facebook

In a town of 360 people, running a café with a focus on pastries and plant-based dishes might seem like a challenge, but for Tracy Kelly-Wilcox, it's a natural fit. With a 30-year career spent in some of Canada's most acclaimed kitchens, Tracy is passionate about contributing to the province's food scene and working with regional and seasonal ingredients.

Originally from Regina, Tracy moved to Ottawa in the 1980s and completed a culinary training program and apprenticeship. From there, she worked at restaurants including Bistro 990 in Toronto and Sooke Harbour House in British Columbia. She moved to Imperial in 2010 to be closer to family, and says that living in rural Saskatchewan has given her an appreciation for the production side of the food industry.

Tracy started a catering business, Pulse Catering, which turned into Grain & Pulse in 2017. At Grain & Pulse the menu features seasonal Prairie ingredients with a plant-forward focus, including staples like lentils and wild rice. There's always a grain bowl and a pulse plate on the weekly lunch menu, plus sandwiches, salads, and brunch fare. Tracy is also a Red Seal pastry chef and bakes European-style pastries daily, including Danishes that are both pretty and delicious. Once a month she hosts a supper club with a set menu, which allows her to put her restaurant experience to the test.

Located in an old house converted into a bakery, Grain & Pulse is the perfect setting for spending an afternoon chatting with friends. It's an inviting, warm space that serves as both the go-to spot in Imperial and a favourite stop for travellers on Highway 2, and it's not hard to see why. The combination of Tracy's expertise and plant-forward focus is unique in rural Saskatchewan, providing a refreshing take on how to highlight the bountiful ingredients the province has to offer.

Grain & Pulse's Chickpea Pancakes with Sautéed Greens Filling and Lemon Yogurt

—

» MAKES 4–6 SERVINGS
» TIME: 45 MINUTES
» GLUTEN-FREE + VEGAN
(OPTION)

Chickpea Pancakes

2 cups chickpea flour*

½ tsp sea salt

½ tsp onion powder

A pinch of ground
cardamom

2 cups water, at room
temperature

2 Tbsp canola oil

Lemon Yogurt

½ cup plain Greek yogurt**

2 Tbsp freshly squeezed
lemon juice

Sautéed Greens Filling

2 Tbsp olive oil

3 small shallots, sliced

2 garlic cloves, minced

½ tsp ground cumin

¼ tsp paprika (any type)

¼ tsp dried thyme

¼ tsp sea salt

A pinch of ground black
pepper

A pinch of dried chilies
(optional)

½ cup cooked chickpeas,
rinsed and drained

½ cup chopped walnuts

½ cup halved cherry
tomatoes

1 (10 oz/300 g) package
frozen chopped spinach,
thawed and squeezed
dry***

2 Tbsp freshly squeezed
lemon juice

1 Tbsp grated lemon zest

Pulses are one of Saskatchewan's main crops. This recipe highlights one of them, chickpeas, in two creative ways: used whole in the filling and ground as flour. The pancakes have a touch of cardamom, which provides a warm, earthy flavour, and are topped with a savoury sautéed greens filling and fresh, creamy lemon yogurt. Tracy notes that this recipe is versatile and can be made sweet or savoury, depending on the ingredients in season. Try topping the golden pancakes with mushrooms and roasted red bell peppers or fresh berries and Greek yogurt—either way, it's a filling plant-based dish, ideal for brunch or lunch. Note that you should let the spinach thaw out overnight before you use it.

CHICKPEA PANCAKES

1. Whisk together the flour, salt, onion powder, and cardamom in a medium bowl. Make a well in the centre of the mixture and add the water and oil. Whisk together until the batter is smooth and well combined. Cover the bowl with plastic wrap and let sit at room temperature for a minimum of 15 minutes, and up to a maximum of 1 hour, to hydrate the flour. While it sits, prepare the other components.

LEMON YOGURT

1. Stir the yogurt and lemon juice together in a small bowl. Refrigerate, uncovered, until you're ready to serve the pancakes.

SAUTÉED GREENS FILLING

1. Heat the oil in a large frying pan over medium heat. Add the shallots and garlic, and cook, stirring regularly, until the shallots begin to soften, about 5 minutes.
2. Mix in the cumin, paprika, thyme, salt, pepper, and dried chilies (if using). Add the chickpeas and walnuts, and stir to coat with the spices. Cook the mixture, stirring regularly, just until the chickpeas and walnuts begin to soften, 3–5 minutes. Then place the tomatoes in the centre of the pan and cook until they start to render their juices, about 2 minutes.
3. Add the spinach, lemon juice, and zest, and stir to combine. Cover the pan with a lid and let it cook until all the ingredients are heated through, 2–3 minutes. Transfer the filling to a medium bowl and cover with aluminum foil or a lid so that it stays warm while you are cooking the pancakes.

1. Heat 1½ to 2 tsp of canola oil in a large frying pan over medium-high heat. (You can use the same pan you used for the filling—no need to wash it first.) Use a silicone brush to spread the oil around evenly, adding more if needed to ensure the pan is evenly coated.

2. Using a ½-cup measuring scoop, drop ½ cup of pancake batter into the pan. Tilt the pan from side to side, to help the batter spread out into an even circle, about 6 inches in diameter. Fry the pancake until brown and crispy on the bottom side, 2–3 minutes, and then flip it over and continue cooking it on the other side until golden and cooked through, 1–2 more minutes. Place the cooked pancake on a plate lined with paper towel, and repeat with the remaining batter. Be sure to re-oil the pan between each pancake. The batter should make 4–6 pancakes.

3. Portion the pancakes onto individual plates and top with a generous scoop of the sautéed greens filling and a dollop of the lemon yogurt. Serve immediately.

*Look for chickpea flour in the natural foods section at the grocery store or at your local organic or bulk foods store.

**To make this recipe vegan, use a dairy-free yogurt substitute, or omit the lemon yogurt topping altogether.

***The spinach should be thawed in the fridge overnight. When you are ready to start the recipe, put it in a sieve set over a bowl and squeeze it firmly with your hands to remove excess liquid.

Tips:

» Do not substitute other oils for the canola oil in the pancake batter. Canola oil works best with chickpea flour. Other oils may produce varying results.

» The cooking method for the sautéed greens filling moves quite quickly, so prior to starting that portion of the method, cut and measure all the filling ingredients so that they are ready to go when you need them.

1155 101st Street
North Battleford,
SK S9A 0Z5
(306) 445-8711
facebook.com/
danishhomebakery

DANISH HOME BAKERY

Andy Thiell's family has a history in the baking business that dates back to 1962, when his grandparents, Anne and August Thiell, moved to North Battleford from Saskatoon and bought the former McConnell's Bakery, which had been operating in the space since 1949.

Andy says the story goes that his grandpa changed the name from McConnell's to Nor-Wood, because the bakery was located north of the woods. Nor-Wood Bakery quickly became a fixture in the Battlefords area, and eventually Andy's parents, Bernard and Therese, began working there, too. They expanded the list of offerings with items like wedding cakes, and Bernard established relationships with local restaurants and grocers who began stocking Nor-Wood's goods. Andy and his siblings all worked alongside their parents in the bakery when they were growing up, making deliveries and taking turns on the midnight shift with their dad to prepare the next day's dough.

In 1988, the family sold the bakery, after 26 years in the business. During that time, Andy had been working at various restaurants in town, including his own, Thirsty's Diner, where he met his wife, Patty. He had sworn off bakeries for good by that point, but eventually he found himself back at his roots, working in bakeries at various grocery stores in North Battleford. When customers kept coming in and saying how great it was to see the Thiell family back in the bakery business, Andy felt that perhaps it was time to open his own. Meanwhile, Nor-Wood Bakery had gone bankrupt under the new ownership, and the Danish Home Bakery, located just down the street, moved into the building in order to expand. When the Danish Home Bakery came up for sale in 1998, Andy and Patty purchased it, in partnership with Bernard and Therese, bringing the family and bakery full circle.

Being back in the original location brought back many memories for the Thiells—they even found Nor-Wood Bakery documents in the basement crawl space. Andy persuaded his dad to come in and help with the night bake again, and Andy and Patty's kids all worked at the bakery while they were growing up too, learning the ropes and helping with deliveries and preparation.

Today, the Danish Home Bakery is still very much a family-oriented place, as Andy's brother Joe works alongside him, and their mom, Therese, now in her 80s, still comes in to assist with the morning shift. They are as busy as ever with popular favourites like cream horns, breads, cookies, and their pies, which still feature Grandma Anne's original pie crust recipe. The bakery is certainly a mainstay for the Battlefords area, as the Thiells supply local restaurants, schools, grocery stores, and the hospital.

People often stop by the bakery to reminisce as they pick up a treat, and to this day Andy still hears customers say that his dad made their wedding cake. It's this sentiment that makes the bakery stand out, and for many customers, a visit to Danish Home Bakery is also a trip down memory lane, where homemade goodies bring back cherished memories of the past.

The outside of Nor-Wood Bakery, circa 1962, showing a new sign made for the business in the shape of a cake. The sign reads "Nor-Wood Bakery Bread - Cakes - Pastry."

Danish Home Bakery's Flax and Oatmeal Cookies

—

» MAKES ABOUT 30 COOKIES
» TIME: 1 HOUR

1 cup all-purpose flour
½ cup quick oats
¼ cup milled or ground flaxseed
1 Tbsp whole flaxseed
½ tsp baking powder
½ tsp baking soda
½ tsp sea salt
¾ cup salted butter, at room temperature
⅓ cup granulated sugar
⅓ cup lightly packed brown sugar
2 large eggs
1 Tbsp vanilla extract

Danish Home Bakery sells 15 different types of cookies, including these, which feature two Saskatchewan crops: flaxseed and oats. The recipe uses both ground and whole flaxseed, and was inspired by a cookie from a summer camp that Andy and Patty's kids attended when they were younger. They recreated the recipe back at the bakery, and it has been popular ever since. The whole flaxseeds add a delightful crunch and nutty flavour to the cookies, which are soft and chewy on the inside with a perfectly crispy outer edge. Pair them with hot coffee or a cold glass of milk, and you're set for dunking.

1. Preheat the oven to 350°F (180°C). Line three baking sheets with parchment paper.
2. Place the flour, oats, milled and whole flaxseed, baking powder, baking soda, and salt in a medium bowl. Mix together to combine.
3. Place the butter and both sugars in a separate medium bowl. Using a handheld electric mixer, beat the butter and sugar on medium speed until fully combined, about 3 minutes.
4. Add the eggs and vanilla extract to the butter and sugar and beat until the mixture is smooth, 2–3 minutes.
5. Add the dry ingredients about ½ cup at a time, beating on low speed after each addition until fully incorporated. Scrape down the sides of the bowl and then beat on high speed for 10 seconds.
6. Using a #40 trigger ice-cream scoop (1½–2 Tbsp of dough per scoop), drop the cookie dough onto the baking sheets with 1½ inches between each cookie.
7. You'll need to bake these in batches. Bake the first two trays on the middle two racks of the oven until nicely browned, 10–12 minutes. At the halfway point, rotate the pans to ensure they bake evenly.
8. Remove the cookies from the oven and let cool on the baking sheets for 5 minutes. Then use a metal spatula to transfer them to a wire cooling rack to cool completely. Bake the final tray while the first batch of cookies are cooling.

Tip: Note that with two pans in the oven, the cookies will take 12 minutes, and with one pan in the oven, they should take closer to 10 minutes.

Saskatoon

—

Saskatoon has been home my entire life, the place I was born and raised, and no matter where I go, it will always be home. I love that it feels like a big city in some ways and a small town in others—a sentiment that is often extended to the province as a whole—and that by driving just 20 minutes in any direction, I can quickly find myself surrounded by natural Prairie landscape.

As a teenager, I had grand plans to leave the province when I graduated from high school. Those plans were rather ambitious and included a year-long backpacking trip to Europe, in which I intended to prance around from one country to the next, drinking wine with my best friend. Though this never happened, later on, when I did spend time travelling to and visiting other parts of Canada and the world, I realized how much I truly loved the city and province I call home.

I know I am not alone in this experience. In many of the interviews I conducted for this book, chefs, bakers, and business owners alike spoke about moving away but eventually returning to the community where they grew up, after realizing it was exactly where they wanted to be. There's something about being away that makes you long for the space of open and endless Prairie, or appreciate the experience of running into someone you know every time you go out. When you return to your roots, there's a comfort in understanding that although you may have changed, your hometown, in many ways, has not.

For this reason, many establishments in Saskatoon—including those featured in this chapter—hold a sense of home for me. Certain establishments I've frequented for years have become places that I feel like I know, as if they're an old friend. On Broadway Avenue, for instance, there are coffee shops where I've spent long afternoons studying and writing, there's a certain gelato shop that I visit more regularly than I care to admit, and there's a local burger joint that my husband and I often get takeout from on Friday nights at the end of a long week.

Similarly, going downtown in Saskatoon means passing by the red double-decker bus turned ice cream shop, where I worked during summers in university. Seeing the bus reminds me of hot, sticky summer days spent peering out the window, snooping on the downtown happenings and chatting with regulars. On days when the line extended down the block, inside the bus we'd scoop ice cream cone after ice cream cone, shouting orders through the window over the background music. The bus is a landmark familiar to many, and whenever I pass by, I can't help but think of how for me it was once more than an ice cream shop—a place where lively conversations happened and friendships were made.

Within our communities, beloved local establishments often come to define "home." In recent years, many new favourites have joined that list, with restaurants and cafés popping up all across the landscape. As business owners and chefs moved back to the province—or moved into it for the first time—they brought with them fresh ideas and talent, helping to push forward Saskatchewan's emerging food scene. In Saskatoon alone, evidence of the culinary growth is everywhere. I love the diversity of establishments in this city and the growing combination of tried-and-true mainstays with refreshing options. As Saskatoon attests, a dynamic food scene often plays a key role in shaping the energy and personality of a given neighbourhood and can truly transform a city, building culture and community in exciting, vibrant ways.

ODD COUPLE RESTAURANT

228 20th Street West
Saskatoon, SK S7M 0W9
(306) 668-8889
oddcouple.ca

Odd Couple has cemented itself as a favourite spot in Saskatoon, bridging Prairie ingredients and flavours with Cantonese, Vietnamese, and Japanese ones. It's a personal favourite for my family, too; a place we frequent for its delicious tomato pad Thai and crispy vegan spring rolls.

Opened in 2014, Odd Couple is owned by Andy and Rachel Yuen and Andy's mom, Jane. The Yuen family immigrated to Canada in 1996 and initially settled in Wynyard, where Andy's uncle owned a restaurant. They later moved to and operated Chinese restaurants in Lanigan and Warman. Rachel is from Guangzhou, China, and came to Saskatchewan to study accounting at the University of Regina.

Andy hadn't planned on opening a restaurant, but he decided to take the leap after being approached about the possibility by Curtis Olson, a long-time friend and owner of the Two Twenty, where Odd Couple is housed. Andy's vision was to create a contemporary setting where people could enjoy Asian-inspired food alongside a cocktail or craft beer. Months later, Odd Couple was born, named after Andy's relationship with his dad, Sam, as the two were often at odds about the restaurant's design. Sam managed the kitchen with Jane until his death in 2019.

Odd Couple's menu is largely influenced by Andy and Rachel's travels through Asia and North America, and it has gained a reputation for being incredibly well-curated. In 2021, Odd Couple was featured on Food Network Canada's *Big Food Bucket List*, which was a proud moment for the Yuens. Andy says he's grateful to have grown up in the hospitality industry and is keen to build on his family's experiences. His ultimate goal is to change perceptions around Asian food and encourage people to try something new by merging traditional dishes with local flavours and ingredients. I'd say Odd Couple is certainly onto something, and it's clear YXE agrees.

Odd Couple's Vietnamese Lemongrass Beef Stew

—

This stew is from the restaurant's "Travels with Odd Couple" menu, which they launched during the COVID-19 pandemic as a way for customers to experience travel through food. First stop was Vietnam, where chef Ivan Ly grew up. Ivan remembers enjoying beef stew in Ho Chi Minh City, where it's typically served with rice noodles or a baguette. He recreated the stew at Odd Couple, and Andy notes that, due to its popularity, it soon moved to their regular fall and winter menu. The stew is hearty, warming, and satisfying, with slow-cooked beef and carrots in a broth that is subtly sweet from the cinnamon.

» MAKES 2–3 SERVINGS
» TIME: 1 HOUR 30 MINUTES + 30 MINUTES–OVERNIGHT TO MARINATE
» GLUTEN-FREE

Lemongrass Beef Stew

1 (2 lb) beef shank, cut into 1½-inch cubes
3½ Tbsp canola oil
10 cherry tomatoes, halved
4 (each ¼-inch thick) slices of fresh ginger
2 garlic cloves, minced
1 shallot, sliced
¼ cup tomato paste
1 stalk of lemongrass, finely diced*
1 stalk of cinnamon
1 whole star anise
4 cups water
2 large carrots, sliced into 1½-inch rounds
1 Tbsp Oriental Beef Spices Seasoning**
1 tsp sea salt
1 tsp brown sugar
Chopped Thai basil and sliced raw white onions, for garnish (optional)
Jasmine rice, rice noodles, or a baguette, for serving (use rice or rice noodles for gluten-free version)

Marinade

¼ cup Oriental Beef Spices Seasoning**
2 garlic cloves, minced
1 shallot, sliced
1 stalk of lemongrass, finely diced*

1. Place the beef cubes in a medium bowl and add all the marinade ingredients. Stir to combine, ensuring all of the cubes are evenly covered. Cover the bowl tightly with plastic wrap and place it in the fridge to marinate for at least 30 minutes, or up to overnight.
2. Once the beef is done marinating, remove it from the fridge and let it sit at room temperature for 10 minutes.
3. Place the oil in a large wok or medium-sized pot over high heat. Add the tomatoes, ginger, garlic, and shallot, and lightly brown, 1–2 minutes.
4. Stir in the tomato paste. Cook for 1 minute and then add the beef, lemongrass, cinnamon stalk, and star anise. Cook, stirring regularly, until the meat is browned on all sides, 2–3 minutes in total.
5. Stir in the water and bring to a boil. Once the water begins to boil, turn the heat to medium-low, cover the pot, and let the stew cook for 40 minutes. Stir it occasionally to ensure all sides of the beef are submerged in the water mixture at some point so that they cook evenly. After 40 minutes, the beef should be about 50–60 percent tender, but not fully cooked.
6. Add the carrots and cook the stew, still on medium-low heat and covered, until the beef and carrots are tender and cooked through, 40 minutes. By this point the meat should have passed the recommended internal temperature of 160°F (71°C). While it's cooking, stir every 5 to 10 minutes to ensure the stew does not stick to the bottom of the pot. If needed, you can turn the heat to low so that it does not stick.
7. Add the seasoning, salt, and sugar. Stir to combine. Adjust the seasoning to taste.
8. Prior to serving, remove the cinnamon stalk and star anise from the stew.
9. Serve the stew in individual bowls. Garnish with chopped Thai basil and sliced raw white onions (if using), along with your choice of jasmine rice, rice noodles, or a baguette.

*To prepare a lemongrass stalk, cut off the root end and then peel off the tough outside layers to reveal the tender inside part. Cut off and discard the top green part of the stalk. Slice the white part of the stalk (similarly to cutting a green onion), and then dice it finely.

**Oriental Beef Spices Seasoning is a dry spice mix. Its Vietnamese name is Gia Vị Nấu Bò Kho. Look for it in the international section of the grocery store or in an Asian grocery store. It is typically in the Vietnamese/Thai spice section and may also be labelled Oriental Beef Spices or Oriental Beef Stew Spices.

Tip: The liquid part of this stew is more like a broth than a sauce, but if you prefer a thicker stew, you can thicken it after adding the last spices in step 7. Combine 1 tsp of cornstarch with ¾ cup water in a small bowl, and stir until the cornstarch is completely dissolved. Add the mixture to the stew, and stir together to combine. Let the stew simmer gently on low heat, stirring occasionally, until the desired consistency is reached.

101 20th Street West
Saskatoon, SK S7M 0W7
(306) 242-0116
picaro.ca

PICARO COCKTAILS & TACOS

Picaro is an ideal place to hunker down and spend an evening indulging in your fair share of nachos, tostadas, and handcrafted margaritas. With industrial décor, dim lighting, and dark tones, the restaurant has a moody and sexy atmosphere, which pairs perfectly with their killer cocktail program. The menu focuses on offering a steady mix of familiar favourites and traditional dishes, combining locally sourced ingredients with ingredients from Mexico. Think Saskatchewan mustard on a taco, mezcal tasting flights, and rice and beans but with local wild rice and chickpeas. It's Latin American–inspired soul food, but with a Prairie take—and it works.

Picaro opened in 2017 and is part of Taste Hospitality Group, owned by Carmen and Brad Hamm. Born and raised in Saskatoon, the couple are avid foodies and travellers who wanted to contribute to the city's growing food scene by opening restaurants similar to those they sought out while travelling. Their first restaurant, the beloved UNA Pizza + Wine, opened in 2016. Taste now includes Cohen's Beer Republic, which is Picaro's sister restaurant; the Cure, an artisanal butcher shop; and catering services.

Before opening Picaro, Carmen and Brad visited Mexico City to learn about the food scene there and its history. They wanted to ensure they were honouring Latin American traditions, and they brought what they learned home to executive chef Steve Squier, who spent a year researching and crafting the menu. At the heart of their food and service philosophy is a belief in transparency, evident in their open kitchen and the quality of local ingredients they use. The carefully curated menu and space give Picaro a distinct big-city feel that is cozy and intimate at the same time—which is exactly what Carmen and Brad were aiming for.

Picaro's Northern Pike Fish Tacos

—

» MAKES 4–6 SERVINGS
» TIME: 1 HOUR 30 MINUTES
» GLUTEN-FREE (OPTION)

Pico de Gallo

5 medium garden or
vine-ripened tomatoes,
diced small
1 medium white onion,
diced small
1 medium jalapeño pepper
1 bunch cilantro
3 limes
1½ tsp kosher salt or sea salt

Chipotle Mayo

4 cups mayonnaise
1 chipotle chili in adobo
sauce
1 lime

Avocado Mousse

1 large ripe avocado
½ cup whipping (35%)
cream*
½ tsp kosher salt or sea salt
2 limes

Northern Pike Fish Tacos

2 large (each 11–18 oz)
northern pike fillets,
deboned and skinless**
2 cups canola oil
8–10 small corn or flour
tortillas (use corn tortillas
for gluten-free option)
1 cup cornmeal
2 tsp kosher salt or sea salt
1 tsp ground black pepper
1½ cups shredded napa
cabbage
Hot sauce, lime wedges,
or microgreens (optional)

This recipe is by Picaro's executive chef Steve Squier, who worked at Elk Ridge Resort in Waskesiu and the Delta Bessborough Hotel in Saskatoon before joining Taste Hospitality Group. These fish tacos have been on Picaro's menu since day one, and feature northern pike (jackfish), which Steve sources directly from Saskatchewan's north. Lightly coated in a crispy cornmeal crust, the fish is complemented by three tasty condiments: pico de gallo, chipotle mayo, and avocado mousse, all of which can be enjoyed with a variety of other dishes. This recipe is a perfect use for freshly caught northern pike and pairs well with a cold beer or a good old shot of mezcal.

PICO DE GALLO

1. Place the tomatoes and onions in a medium bowl.
2. Remove the stem from the jalapeño pepper and cut it in half lengthwise. For less spice, discard the ribs and seeds. Slice the jalapeño into thin strips, and then dice it very finely. Add it to the bowl.
3. Roughly chop the cilantro, including the stems, being careful not to overchop so that it does not bruise. Add three-quarters of the cilantro to the bowl, and set the remainder aside.
4. Squeeze the limes and add the lime juice and salt to the bowl, and stir to combine. Set it aside until you are ready to serve the tacos.

CHIPOTLE MAYO

1. Using a blender or food processor fitted with a steel blade, blend the mayonnaise and chipotle pepper on high speed until completely smooth.
2. Squeeze the lime and add the lime juice to the mayonnaise and chipotle mixture. Blend again until all the ingredients are well combined and the mixture is smooth. Transfer to a small serving bowl and refrigerate until you are ready to serve the tacos.
3. Leftover chipotle mayo can be stored in an airtight container or squeeze bottle in the fridge for up to 1 week.

AVOCADO MOUSSE

1. Cut the avocado in half and discard the pit. Using a spoon, scoop the avocado flesh into a blender or food processor. Add the cream and salt.
2. Squeeze the limes and add the lime juice to the avocado and cream.

3. Purée on high speed until smooth. Transfer to a bowl and cover with plastic wrap until you are ready to serve the tacos. Make sure the plastic touches the surface of the mousse, which will help prevent it from turning brown.

NORTHERN PIKE FISH TACOS

1. Cut the fish into strips about 1-inch wide, and pat them dry with a paper towel.
2. Place the oil in a large frying pan or saucepan over medium-high heat. The oil should be about 1-inch deep. Warm the oil to about 350°F (180°C), using an instant-read thermometer to check the temperature.
3. While the oil is heating up, heat a medium frying pan over medium heat. Once the pan is hot, place the tortillas in the pan, one by one, and heat both sides for about 45 seconds per side. Wrap the hot tortillas in a clean dishtowel to keep them warm.
4. Mix the cornmeal, salt, and pepper together in a shallow dish large enough to hold the fish, and place the fish strips, one at a time, in the cornmeal. Roll them around to coat all sides.
5. Using tongs, place 4–5 pieces of coated fish in the hot oil, being careful not to splash yourself with oil. Cook the fish for 2 minutes on one side, and then flip and cook for an additional 1–2 minutes on the other side. Once the fish is cooked through and crispy, remove them with tongs or a slotted spoon and place them on a plate covered with paper towel to drain it. Repeat the process until all the fish is cooked. You may have to bring the oil back to temperature between batches.

TO ASSEMBLE

1. Place 2 warmed tortillas on a plate. Spread or drizzle about 1 Tbsp of chipotle mayo on each tortilla, leaving a small mayo-free border all round the tortilla.
2. Add a small handful of cabbage to each tortilla, scattering it in a line down the centre of each one.
3. Place 1–2 strips of fish on top of the cabbage.
4. Drizzle a little bit more chipotle mayo overtop of the fish.
5. Spoon a generous amount of pico de gallo on top of the fish, and place about 1 tsp of avocado mousse on either side of the fish on the tortilla. Top with some of the remaining chopped cilantro.
6. Repeat the process with the rest of the tortillas, and garnish with hot sauce, lime wedges, or microgreens (if using). Serve immediately.

*For a dairy-free version of the avocado mousse, substitute a non-dairy milk like coconut milk or oat milk for the cream.
**You can use fresh or frozen fish for this recipe. If using frozen, be sure to thaw it overnight in the fridge first.

Sourcing tip: For where to find northern pike fillets, see the Sourcing Local Guide (page 288).

BABA'S HOMESTYLE PEROGIES

720B 51st Street East
Saskatoon, SK S7K 4K4
(306) 933-4280
babasperogies.com

Saskatchewanians have a long-standing love affair with perogies, loaded with all manner of toppings from sour cream and bacon to fried onions and mushroom sauce. Visit any street fair, fundraising night, or community event, and there's a good chance you'll see them on the menu. The province's enthusiasm for perogies extends far beyond any other: it is the home of Canada's only drive-thru perogy restaurant, Baba's Homestyle Perogies. In fact, owner Rob Engel claims he's never heard of anything like it *anywhere*.

In October of 2020, Baba's was featured on Food Network Canada's *Big Food Bucket List,* and nobody from the show had heard of another present-day perogy drive-thru either. Rob's theory is that people in Saskatchewan want to eat perogies but don't want to go out in the cold, and the perogy drive-thru offers the perfect solution to this dilemma. Whatever the reason, Baba's has its work cut out, making over 2 million perogies annually (an average of 10,000 to 15,000 perogies per day, depending on the season), all hand-pinched by their dedicated team.

The original baba of the operation, Alice Joyal, started the business in 1984, after making perogies for family and friends for years. Rob; his wife, Chelsea; and their family are the third owners of the business, and when they took over in 2006, Rob says it was a dream come true. Both Rob and Chelsea have fond memories of eating homemade perogies when they were growing up, and the baba in their family today is Chelsea's mom, who is always happy to show them how to cook traditional Ukrainian dishes.

When the family first purchased the business, the drive-thru was part of the building but not in use. They decided to restore it, and now the drive-thru is a popular convenience, seeing anywhere from 50 to 100 cars per day. Saskatoon actually has a history of perogy drive-thrus that dates back to 1962, when the O&O Drive-in opened on 20th Street West. The original co-owners, Ostap (Ozzie) Nahachewsky and Orest Romanko (the two O's), ran the business with their families, and sold traditional Ukrainian food like perogies and cabbage rolls, along with burgers and ice cream. They also offered catering and take-home goods, in addition to the drive-thru, which had an iconic Ukrainian cross-stitch design painted on the sides of the building.

After a few years the Romanko family left the business, and the Nahachewsky family continued operating it until 1992. Rob often gets asked if there's a connection between Baba's and the O&O, and while the answer is no, they will always be linked by two things: handmade Ukrainian food and, of course, the perogy drive-thru.

At Baba's, there are seven different types of perogies, including potato and cheddar, sauerkraut, Saskatoon berry, and dairy-free potato and onion. The recipes haven't changed over the years and remain true to their roots. Baba's also offers catering, dine-in, and a freezer section stocked with take-home goods.

Rob notes that customers often have an emotional connection to the food, especially the perogies. My own family is Ukrainian and Hungarian, and no holiday would be complete without my baba's potato perogies, topped with onions, butter, and creamy mushroom gravy.

When you walk into Baba's Perogies you can usually glimpse the staff in the back, filling and pinching perogies with such precision and speed you can barely catch their movements. There's a nostalgic, familiar quality to both the atmosphere and the food, reminiscent of time spent around the table with family, rolling, cutting, and shaping perogies. For many, Baba's provides a window into the past, where tradition lives on, one hand-pinched perogy at a time.

Saskatoon's history of perogie drive-thrus dates back to the O&O Drive-In, which operated at 20th Street West and Avenue L South from 1962 to 1992. This photo is circa 1968.

Baba's Homestyle Perogies' Potato and Cheddar Perogies

—

» MAKES ABOUT 100 PEROGIES

» TIME: 3–4 HOURS* + 1–2 HOURS TO CHILL

Filling

5 lb red potatoes, peeled and diced medium

2 cups finely shredded sharp cheddar cheese

½ tsp ground black pepper

Salt, to taste

Cooked bacon, fried onions, cottage cheese, or fresh or dried dill (optional)**

Dough

2 cups hot water

2 Tbsp canola oil

2 tsp salt

5 ½ cups all-purpose flour***

Garnish

Margarine or butter

Cooked bacon, fried onions, sour cream, or mushroom dill sauce (optional)

This recipe is for Baba's potato and cheddar perogies, which are their most popular item. The perogies are soft, doughy, and filled with cheesy potato goodness, and are best finished with bacon and fried onions, or your favourite perogy topping, of course. Rob notes that it's easy to quickly devour a dozen of these without thinking, and he's even seen customers inhale 30 or more in one sitting. Perogies pair well with farmer sausage and traditional Ukrainian fare like cabbage rolls and mushroom dill sauce. If you're preparing perogies for an upcoming holiday or gathering, they can be made in advance and frozen until needed.

FILLING

1. Place the potatoes in a large pot with enough salted water to cover them, and bring to a boil over high heat. Once it's boiling, turn down the heat to medium and cook the potatoes until they are very soft, 20–25 minutes.

2. Drain the water and transfer the potatoes to a large bowl. Add the cheese and pepper, and then, using a potato masher, mash everything together until the mixture is smooth and all the lumps are removed. (Alternatively, you can use a stand mixer fitted with the paddle attachment for this step, mixing the potatoes on low speed until smooth.)

3. Taste the filling to ensure it is seasoned to your liking. If needed, add a bit of salt or more pepper to taste. If you are using any optional filling additions, add them to the bowl now and mix until they are fully incorporated into the potato mixture.

4. Let the filling cool slightly, then cover the bowl with plastic wrap and refrigerate to chill completely, 1–2 hours. (Alternatively, you can make the filling ahead of time and let it chill in the fridge overnight.)

DOUGH

1. If using a stand mixer: Place the hot water, oil, and salt in the bowl of a stand mixer fitted with the dough hook. Stir to combine and then add the flour. Mix the dough on medium speed until it has formed a solid dough ball, 2–3 minutes. The dough should be smooth and not sticky or wet, so if needed, add about 1 Tbsp more flour at a time to reach the desired consistency.

2. If mixing by hand: Place the hot water, oil, and salt in a large bowl. Stir to combine and then add the flour to the bowl in 3 additions. Mix together with a wooden spoon after each of

the first 2 additions, and then use your hands to mix in the final addition. Once all the flour has been added, knead the dough in the bowl until it is well mixed and forms a solid dough ball, about 5 minutes. The dough should be smooth and not sticky or wet, so if needed, add about 1 Tbsp more flour at a time to reach the desired consistency.

3.   Lightly flour a clean surface and cover 3–4 rimmed baking sheets with clean dishtowels.

4.   Cut off a quarter of the dough, and cover the remaining dough with plastic wrap or a lid while it is not in use. Using well-floured hands, knead the dough 2 to 3 times on a clean surface, dusting with flour as needed.

5.   Use a rolling pin to roll out the dough to an ⅛-inch thickness.

6.   Using a small cup, cookie cutter, or pastry cutter (about 2½ to 3 inches in diameter), cut circles out of the dough. Place the circles on a clean, floured surface, or on the baking sheets. Do not lay them on top of each other as they may stick.

7.   Remove the perogy filling from the fridge. Take 1 dough circle and stretch it in your hand to create a small oval-shaped pocket. Hold the dough in one hand and fill it with about 1 Tbsp of filling. You may need to use less than 1 Tbsp depending on how large your dough circles are. Be careful not to overfill, as it will be difficult to seal the perogy. Use your finger to guide the potato filling inside as you fold the dough in half around the filling, pinching firmly but gently along the edges with your thumb and index finger. Ensure no filling is coming out of the sides and that the perogy is well sealed.

8.   Lay the completed perogy on one of the dishtowel-lined rimmed baking sheets. Be sure to space the completed perogies evenly apart so they are not overlapping.

9.   Repeat with the remaining dough, working with one quarter of the dough at a time. You can work any dough scraps back into the dough to incorporate them.

10. The perogies can be cooked immediately or frozen. To freeze the perogies, first freeze them overnight on the baking sheets, uncovered, and then transfer them to large freezer storage bags. They can be kept frozen for up to 6 months and then cooked directly from frozen.

TO COOK

1.   Fill a large pot with water and bring it to a rolling boil over high heat.

2.   Add 24–36 fresh or frozen perogies to the pot and stir gently, ensuring that the perogies do not stick to each other. Be careful not to overcrowd the pot.

3.   Cook the perogies at a rolling boil. Once they float to the top of the water, wait 1 more minute, and then, using a slotted spoon, remove them from the water. The total cooking time is 3–4 minutes for fresh perogies, or about 7 minutes for frozen.

4.   Place the cooked perogies in a large casserole dish with a generous helping of butter to ensure they do not stick together. If you are

cooking several dozen perogies at one time, keep the cooked perogies covered and/or place them in the oven preheated to its lowest temperature. Once all the perogies are cooked, they can be served immediately with any optional garnishes. (Alternatively, you can transfer them to a large frying pan and fry them over medium heat in butter until golden brown, 3–5 minutes.)

*The time variation accounts for how many people are involved in the perogy pinching. Many hands make light work!
**These options can be added to the perogy filling to taste. If you're adding cooked bacon or fried onions, try using ½ cup to 1 cup. For a potato and cottage cheese filling, omit the shredded cheddar cheese and use 6 cups dry cottage cheese. Fresh or dried dill can be added at about 2 Tbsp per batch.
***When measuring the flour, make sure to spoon it and not pack it tightly in the measuring cup.

Tip: You may have a little bit of perogy filling left over, especially if you added any optional additions to the filling. Leftover filling makes for great whipped potatoes, or can be added to dishes like a casserole or shepherd's pie.

117-123 Avenue B South
Saskatoon, SK S7M 5X6
(306) 281-8000
tastebotte.com

BOTTÉ CHAI BAR

Botté Chai Bar is a breath of fresh air in today's busy world, with a calming atmosphere, reminiscent of an oasis, inviting you to slow down and find a moment of peace. It's a humble space that is home to one of the province's best-kept secrets: the only Persian teahouse and kitchen of its kind in all of Saskatchewan.

Owner Parviz Yazdani is originally from Iran and moved to Saskatchewan in the 1980s. For years, his family dreamed of opening a space that would bring Persian culture to Saskatoon, and Parviz credits his mom, Behshid Zehtab, and her passion for cooking as the driving force that brought Botté to life in 2018.

Primarily a teahouse, Botté's signature house-brewed chai features notes of orange blossom, rose petal, and cardamom, which combine to create a deliciously warm and complex spice palate. The chai is a family recipe and serves as the perfect accompaniment to one of their 30 desserts, including favourites like baklava and saffron rice pudding. In 2020 Botté added their Persian Kitchen, which operates out of the Local Kitchen's commercial space next door. The menu offers savoury dishes like barley aush and plum chicken, with plenty of gluten-free and vegetarian options, too.

Botté's décor incorporates elements of both a traditional Iranian teahouse and a Persian garden, with ornate lights from Turkey, a plant wall, and a comfy booth lining the entire seating area, complete with cushions in colourful, bold prints. Parviz wanted the design to be both welcoming and versatile, inviting people from all walks of life to enjoy a meal or cozy up with a cup of tea. The ambience is truly distinctive, offering a tranquil refuge alongside home-cooked Persian food, right in Saskatoon's Riversdale neighbourhood.

Botté Chai Bar's Adasi

—

» MAKES 6–8 SERVINGS
» TIME: 2 HOURS 30 MINUTES
   + 1 HOUR TO SOAK
» GLUTEN-FREE (OPTION)
   + VEGAN

Adasi

1½ cups dried brown lentils
2 Tbsp canola or olive oil
1 medium white onion,
   diced small
5 garlic cloves, minced
¼ cup + 2 Tbsp tomato
   paste, divided
1½ tsp ground turmeric
1½ tsp ground cumin
1½ tsp Persian allspice
   (advieh)*
9 cups water
3 medium yellow potatoes,
   peeled and diced small
2 Tbsp freshly squeezed
   lemon juice
¾ Tbsp sea salt
½ tsp ground black pepper
½ cup crispy fried onions
   (optional, for garnish;
   omit for gluten-free
   option)

Garlic Mint Oil

¼ cup olive oil
2 garlic cloves, minced
2 Tbsp dried mint

Adasi is a Persian lentil soup commonly served for breakfast, and this particular recipe is by Botté's chef, Diana Gray. At Botté, adasi is on the brunch menu and features Saskatchewan lentils simmered in a broth of tomato and aromatic spices until the lentils become soft and tender, making the adasi thick, almost like a stew. It's a hearty dish that makes for a great family-style meal, with intricate yet subtle flavours that are earthy and savoury. Serve adasi alongside eggs for breakfast, or with sourdough or flatbread as a stand-alone meal.

ADASI

1. Place the lentils in a medium bowl with enough water to cover them, ensuring they are fully immersed. Place the bowl on the counter to soak for 1 hour.
2. Once the lentils are done soaking, heat the oil in a medium pot over medium heat. Add the onion and sauté until soft and lightly browned, about 5 minutes.
3. Mix in the garlic, 2 Tbsp of the tomato paste, the turmeric, cumin, and allspice. Sauté until all the ingredients are combined and aromatic, 5 minutes.
4. Drain the soaked lentils and add them to the pot, followed by the water and then the potatoes. Stir to combine. Turn up the heat to high and bring the adasi to a boil.
5. Once it's boiling, turn down the heat to medium, cover the pot, and let it cook, stirring occasionally, for 1½ hours. After 1½ hours, the lentils should be soft and the mixture should have a thick stew-like consistency.
6. Add the remaining ¼ cup of tomato paste, the lemon juice, salt, and pepper and stir to combine. If needed, add more lemon juice, salt, and/or pepper to taste. Let the adasi cook on medium heat, still covered, for an additional 30 minutes, stirring occasionally.
7. Turn the heat to low and let it simmer, uncovered, while you prepare the garlic mint oil (below).
8. Serve the adasi in a large bowl, family-style, or portion it into individual servings. Top with the garlic mint oil and garnish with crispy fried onions (if using).
9. Leftover adasi can be frozen in an airtight container for up to 3 months. To reheat, add the adasi and a little bit of water to a pot over medium heat, stirring occasionally, until it is completely thawed and cooked through.

GARLIC MINT OIL

1. Heat the oil in a small frying pan over low heat. Add the garlic and mint, and let them cook, stirring regularly, until the mixture is dark green, 3–4 minutes.

*Look for Persian allspice (advieh) in the international section of the grocery store or at a Middle Eastern grocery store. If it proves elusive, you can substitute ½ tsp ground cinnamon and a pinch of ground cardamom.

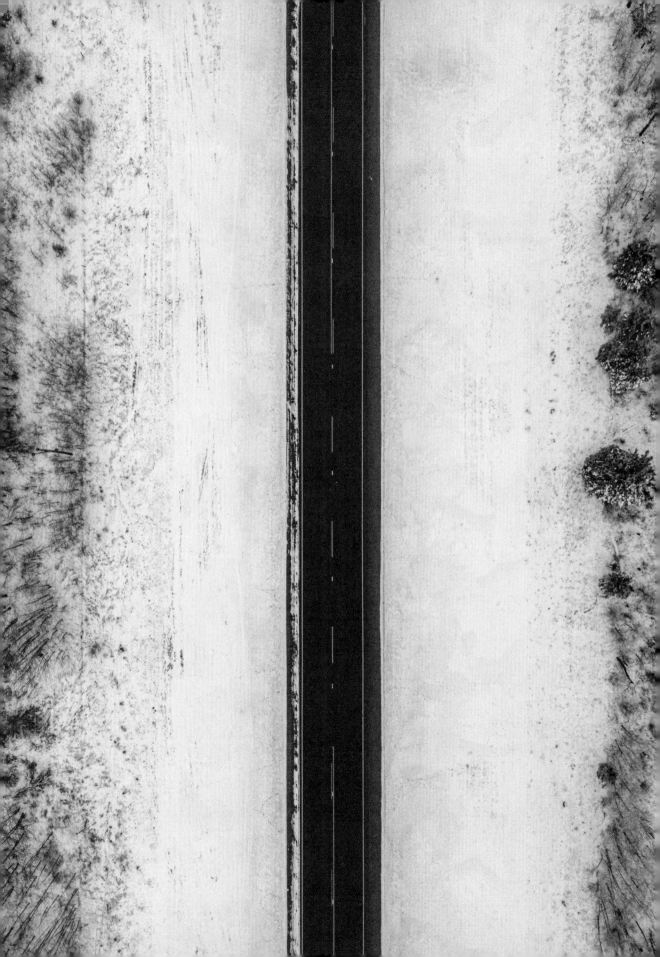

THE NIGHT OVEN BAKERY

216 Avenue D North
Saskatoon, SK S7L 1M6
(306) 500-2350
thenightoven.ca

The Night Oven Bakery is Saskatchewan's only bakery with a flour mill, which they use to grind organic heritage grains like red fife, spelt, einkorn, and rye. With a food philosophy rooted in the slow food movement, owner Bryn Rawlyk is passionate about taking an active role in local food systems, sourcing grain from within a two-hour radius of Saskatoon.

Originally from Saskatoon, Bryn spent years working at bakeries in Montreal and Vancouver, where he gained an understanding of, and appreciation for, the craft. While living in Montreal, he was also involved in a community project to build a wood-fired oven, which was used by locals for baking, cooking, and neighbourhood events. The experience showed him how food can bring people together, and, after moving back home, he became involved with Slow Food Saskatoon. In 2012, Bryn and his wife, Beth, went as local representatives to the Slow Food International Congress in Italy, where Bryn had the opportunity to connect with like-minded bakers from many countries. The experience inspired him to create a bakery that would connect farmer and consumer by crafting wholesome products made with quality, organic ingredients.

Prior to opening the bakery in 2013, Bryn spent a year building its first stone mill and a 9-foot wood-fired brick oven, where many of their items are baked. Everything in the bakery is made from flour that they grind in-house, which results in baked goods that are simple yet exceptional. Sourdough loaves and French-inspired pastries make up the bulk of the menu, but pizza is offered on Friday nights and various specialty items appear throughout the year, like fruitcake for the holidays.

Bryn now also owns Darkside Donuts and Venn Coffee Roasters in Saskatoon, which are just as popular as the Night Oven. It's clear that his commitment to creating food that is thoughtfully tended, from sheaf, to flour, to bread, has struck a chord with customers, both locally and provincially.

The Night Oven Bakery's Square Bread

—

» MAKES 2 LOAVES OF BREAD
» TIME: 2 HOURS +
   3½ HOURS TO RISE +
   8 HOURS–OVERNIGHT FOR
   THE POOLISH TO REST
» VEGAN

Poolish

1 cup all-purpose flour
⅛ tsp active dry yeast
1 cup water, at room
    temperature

Square Bread

6⅔ cups sifted all-purpose
    flour
1⅔ cups whole wheat flour
3½ tsp salt
1 Tbsp active dry yeast
2⅓ cups water, at room
    temperature

When Bryn was testing out bread recipes at home in preparation for the Night Oven's opening, his kids kept requesting that he make "the square bread," as opposed to round sourdough loaves. The name stuck, and so has the bread, which has been on the Night Oven's menu since the beginning. This recipe uses a poolish, which is a type of pre-fermentation that adds flavour and complexity to the bread. It's a simple, classic loaf that's perfect for sandwiches or toast, and it's easy to make at home in a bread tin or loaf pan. Note that you'll need to allow 14 hours from start to finish for this recipe, but much of that time is for resting/rising.

POOLISH

1. Place all the poolish ingredients in a medium bowl and mix together until well combined. Cover the bowl with a clean dishtowel and let the poolish sit on the counter for at least 8 hours, or up to overnight. During this time a slight film may form on top of the poolish, but this is normal. It will be incorporated into the bread dough later.

SQUARE BREAD

1. Once the poolish is done resting, place it in the bowl of a stand mixer fitted with the dough hook or in a large bowl. Add all the bread ingredients to the bowl. If using a stand mixer, mix on the lowest speed until the dough is just combined and wet, 5–10 minutes. If using a regular bowl, mix the dough together with your hands until it is just combined and wet, 5–10 minutes.
2. Let the dough sit in the bowl, uncovered, on the counter for 15 minutes. Then mix it a second time until the consistency is strong, smooth, and stretchy. If you are using a stand mixer, mix it on the lowest speed for about 15 minutes, and if you are using your hands, knead it for about 15 minutes, until the desired consistency is reached.
3. Form the dough into a ball and place it in a lightly oiled bowl. Cover it with a clean dishtowel and let it sit in a warm, draft-free place until it looks puffy and has almost doubled in size, about 2 hours.
4. Place the dough on a clean, lightly floured surface and divide it in two. Shape each half into a ball and let them rest, uncovered, for 20 minutes.
5. Meanwhile, using a pastry or silicone brush, lightly oil the sides and bottoms of two bread tins or loaf pans (canola oil works well).

Note that the size of the pan does not matter too much. Any standard bread tin or loaf pan will work. If you have two different sized pans, you can shape the bread to them accordingly.

6. Take one of the dough balls and flatten it gently into a roughly shaped rectangle. Bring the two long sides together, and roll it into a log, pinching the seam together. Form the log roughly to the length of your bread pan, and then place the dough log in the pan. Repeat the process with the other dough ball.

7. Cover the bread pans with a clean dishtowel and let the dough rise one last time in a warm, draft-free place until it is about 1 inch above the edge of the pan, about 1 hour.

8. Once the dough has risen, preheat the oven to 400°F (200°C).

9. Bake the bread on the centre rack of the oven until golden brown, 40 minutes. If you prefer a lighter crust, leave the bread in for slightly less time, around 35 minutes, or for a crispier, darker crust, leave it in for about 45 minutes.

10. Remove the bread from the oven, and, once it is cool enough to touch, turn it out onto a wire rack. Let the bread cool slightly at room temperature and then slice it and serve immediately.

WANUSKEWIN HERITAGE PARK

RR 4, Penner Road
Saskatoon, SK S7K 3J7
(306) 931-6767
wanuskewin.com

Located in Treaty 6 territory and the Homeland of the Métis, Wanuskewin is a hub of archaeological history, education, and natural beauty. The park is just outside Saskatoon, near Opimihaw Creek and the South Saskatchewan River, and serves as both a local and a global gathering space. It's a place where you can escape into the pull of nature year-round, with walking paths that weave through golden prairie and lush greenery in warmer months, and turn into a frosty, snowy haven come wintertime.

The Cree word *wânaskêwin* translates to English as "seeking peace of mind" or "being at peace with oneself," named for the Indigenous peoples who lived peacefully in the valley for over 6,000 years, until Treaty 6 was signed in 1876. The land was then homesteaded by settlers from 1902 until the 1980s, when archeological excavation of the site began. Over the years there have been many archeological discoveries, including the most northerly documented Medicine Wheel in all of the Great Plains. In 1984, Wanuskewin became a Provincial Heritage Property, followed by a National Historic Site in 1987, and opened as a Heritage Park in 1992.

All of Wanuskewin's initiatives, including their exhibits, programming, and events, are rooted in interpretation, in efforts to learn from and engage with Indigenous peoples in Saskatchewan and their cultures. Wanuskewin is well worth visiting to experience and learn about the dynamic history of Indigenous peoples of the Northern Plains, in a space that is both beautiful and sacred.

Wanuskewin's on-site restaurant and catering services focus on combining traditional Indigenous cuisines with contemporary dishes, and bison and bannock are both key features of the menu. Hearty favourites include Métis Boulettes (bison meatballs with vegetables), their Tatanka Bison Burger, and baked bannock. They source local ingredients whenever possible too, using buns from the Night Oven Bakery in Saskatoon and wild fruit from Boreal Heartland, an Indigenous-owned company in Air Ronge.

A full renovation of the site was completed in 2020, including an expansion of their Interpretive Centre and exhibits, and the addition of a spacious conference and event centre. The building itself is warm and inviting, with wood walls and ceilings that reflect the natural landscape outside. Large picture windows flood the space with soft sunlight year-round and offer breath-taking panoramic views of the river valley. All in all, it's a stunning place to enjoy a meal or take in an event like a guided tour, their annual Kôna Winter Festival, or a Dance Presentation.

The renovation also included the reintroduction of Plains bison to the park, after a 150-year absence from their homelands due to settler interference. In 2019, six female calves from Grasslands National Park and five bison from the United States with ancestral ties to Yellowstone National Park were brought over, and in the spring of 2020, four calves were born. Wanuskewin's senior interpretive guide, Honey Constant, notes that the reintroduction of the bison is an important step in revitalizing what was lost when the bison were driven from the land. The reintroduction is a key piece to reclaiming cultures, languages, and traditions, and helping to restore the grasslands by cultivating a natural habitat for the bison, which came close to extinction in past.

At time of writing, Wanuskewin was on the Tentative List, the first stage in a long process to become a UNESCO World Heritage Site. The nomination is a first for Saskatchewan and speaks to the significance of the work being done there. Whether it's learning about the past, restoring the natural landscape, or sharing experiences through food, education, and cultures, Wanuskewin is planting and nourishing the seeds for a future rooted in connection and understanding.

In December of 2019, six female calves and five bison were brought to Wanuskewin Heritage Park, after a 150-year absence from the grasslands. Four calves were born in the spring of 2020, adding to the herd, which is for conservation purposes.

Wanuskewin's Bison Bannock Pockets with Cranberry Marinara

—

» MAKES 8 BISON BANNOCK POCKETS + 2½ CUPS MARINARA + 2¾ CUPS BBQ SAUCE

» TIME: 2 HOURS 30 MINUTES

This recipe was created by Julie Bear, of Shoal Lake Cree Nation, and Darci McAdam, of Pelican Lake First Nation, both of whom work at Wanuskewin's restaurant. Bison bannock pockets are on Wanuskewin's Mitten Menu, which features warm, handheld items meant to be eaten while hiking the park's trails. The pockets are a cozy, comforting meal, oven-baked and stuffed with a pulled bison filling, and the cranberry marinara is the perfect accompaniment, with a rich jam-like flavour. If needed, you can substitute beef or pork for the bison, or switch out the maple BBQ sauce for your favourite BBQ sauce.

Cranberry Marinara

1 Tbsp olive oil

⅓ cup small-diced carrot

¼ cup small-diced yellow onion

1 garlic clove, minced

2 cups crushed tomatoes

1 Tbsp tomato paste

2½ cups fresh or frozen cranberries

2 Tbsp granulated sugar

1 Tbsp dried oregano

1 Tbsp dried basil

2 Tbsp water

Bison Filling

1 (2 lb) bison roast*

1 tsp sea salt

1 tsp ground black pepper

3 Tbsp vegetable oil

1 cup water

1½ cups maple BBQ sauce (below)**

Maple BBQ Sauce

2 cups ketchup

1 (5½ oz/156 mL) can of tomato paste

⅓ cup apple cider vinegar

¼ cup maple syrup

¼ cup molasses

2 Tbsp Worcestershire sauce

1 tsp paprika (any type is fine)

1 tsp garlic powder

1 tsp dry mustard powder

½ tsp sea salt

½ tsp ground black pepper

A pinch of cayenne pepper

CRANBERRY MARINARA

1. Heat the oil in a medium saucepan over medium heat.
2. Add the carrot, onion, and garlic to the saucepan, and sauté until the onion becomes translucent, about 5 minutes.
3. Stir in the crushed tomatoes and tomato paste. Let the mixture simmer on medium heat for 3 minutes.
4. Add the cranberries, sugar, oregano, basil, and water and bring to a boil over high heat. Once it's boiling, turn the heat to medium and allow it to simmer, uncovered, and stirring regularly, until the cranberries are cooked through and beginning to split open, 15 minutes.
5. Remove the sauce from the heat and blend it on high speed until it is fairly smooth. You can use an immersion blender, stand blender, or food processor for this.
6. Let the cranberry marinara cool at room temperature and then refrigerate, covered, until you are ready to serve the bison bannock pockets. Leftover cranberry marinara can be refrigerated in an airtight container for up to 1 week.

BISON FILLING

1. Preheat the oven to 300°F (150°C).
2. Cut the bison roast into quarters and place them in a medium bowl. Sprinkle the salt and pepper overtop and turn to season all sides.
3. Heat the oil in a large frying pan over medium heat. Add the bison pieces to the pan and lightly sear all sides until just browned, about 5 minutes in total.
4. Pour 1 cup of water into a roasting pan, add the bison, and cover with either a lid or aluminum foil. Cook the bison until it is tender and reaches an internal temperature of 145°F (63°C), 45–50 minutes.
5. Meanwhile, prepare the maple BBQ sauce (below) and then the bannock dough (below).

Bannock

2 cups all-purpose flour
1½ cups whole wheat flour
1½ Tbsp baking powder
1 Tbsp brown sugar
½ tsp sea salt
1½ cups warm water
¼ cup canola oil
Melted butter or olive oil, for brushing (optional)

6. Remove the bison from the oven and let it cool slightly.
7. Using two forks, pull apart the meat to shred it, and place the shredded meat in a medium bowl.
8. Add 1½ cups of the BBQ sauce to the pulled bison, and mix together until well combined.

MAPLE BBQ SAUCE

1. Place all of the sauce ingredients in a medium saucepan. Stir together to combine and then bring to a boil over high heat, stirring occasionally. Once the mixture is boiling, turn the heat to medium-low and allow it to simmer, uncovered, and stirring occasionally, until it has the consistency of BBQ sauce, about 15 minutes. Remove from the heat and let cool.
2. Store any leftover maple BBQ Sauce in an airtight container in the fridge for up to 1 week.

BANNOCK

1. Mix together both flours, the baking powder, sugar, and salt in a large bowl until well combined.
2. Add the water and oil, and knead with your hands until a solid dough forms. It should hold together and not stick to your hands when you touch it. If it is too sticky, add a little bit more flour as needed until it reaches a dough-like consistency.
3. Cover the dough with plastic wrap and allow it to rest for 20 minutes in a warm area.

TO ASSEMBLE

1. Preheat the oven to 375°F (190°C). Line a rimmed baking sheet with parchment paper.
2. Lightly flour a clean surface. Form the bannock dough into a flat disk. Cut the dough into 8 portions, one for each pocket. Keep the dough you are not using covered.
3. Take one dough portion and, using a rolling pin, roll it out into a thin circle, about 7 inches in diameter. Place a heaping ⅓ cup of the bison filling on one half of the bannock circle, leaving ½-inch space from the edge. Using a silicone barbeque brush, brush a little bit of water along the edges of the dough, and then fold the dough over the pulled bison and press down firmly on the edges with a fork to seal it.
4. Using a large spatula, transfer the completed pocket to the prepared baking sheet. Repeat the process until all the dough and filling are used up. To keep the dough from sticking, dust your work surface and rolling pin with flour as you go.
5. Lightly poke a few holes on the top of each pocket with a fork. Using a silicone barbeque brush, lightly brush each pocket with a little bit of melted butter (if using).
6. Bake the pockets on the centre rack of the oven until golden brown and cooked through, 10–15 minutes.
7. Remove the pockets from the oven, let them cool on the pan enough to touch, and then serve immediately with the cranberry marinara on the side for dipping.

*Use a bison round roast, chuck roast, or rib eye roast, which all have a decent ratio of meat to fat. A leaner cut will work but will be difficult to shred. Alternatively, you can substitute a beef or pork roast of equal weight for the bison, if desired.
**The maple BBQ sauce can be substituted with 1½ cups of your favourite BBQ sauce.

Sourcing tip: For where to find bison, see the Sourcing Local Guide (page 279).

AYDEN KITCHEN & BAR

265 3rd Avenue South
Saskatoon, SK S7K 1M3
(306) 954-2590
aydenkitchenandbar.com

Ayden Kitchen & Bar is a pillar of Saskatoon's culinary scene, known for innovative food and cocktail menus that showcase Prairie flavours and ingredients. Opened in 2013, Ayden is part of Grassroots Restaurant Group, which was founded by Dale MacKay and Christopher Cho.

Originally from Ontario, Christopher is a seasoned restaurateur and mixologist, bringing a strong focus on craft cocktails to the Grassroots team. Dale grew up in Saskatoon and began his career in Vancouver restaurants, but eventually ended up in England, working for Michelin Star chef Gordon Ramsay. After spending years working with various Gordon Ramsay restaurants abroad, he moved back to Vancouver and began working with Michelin Star chef Daniel Boulud, which is how he and Christopher met. Dale went on to win the inaugural season of *Top Chef Canada* in 2011, before moving home to Saskatoon.

Dale says his ultimate goal with Ayden was to put Saskatchewan on the map, and he named the restaurant after his son. (These days Ayden himself is a host at Ayden Kitchen & Bar.) Since 2013, Grassroots has grown to include catering services, two other Saskatoon restaurants—Little Grouse on the Prairie, an Italian restaurant; and Sticks and Stones, a Japanese and Korean restaurant—and Avenue Restaurant, which offers contemporary comfort food and cocktails in downtown Regina. In 2021, Grassroots expanded with a second Regina restaurant, DOJO Ramen, which is another iteration of Japanese and Korean food, also in the downtown.

Ayden Kitchen & Bar is housed in a Municipal Heritage Property known as the McLean Block and has a warm industrial feel, with exposed pipes, high ceilings, and vintage hardwood floors from 1912. A large, expansive bar serves as a gorgeous focal point, and the open kitchen is a customer favourite, with many requesting to sit directly in front of the chefs so they can watch the magic happen. Nowadays, the menu is carefully curated by executive chef Benet Hunt, who hails from England and was on *Top Chef Canada* in 2019. He says the menu focuses on dishes that people know and love, but with unexpected and welcome flavours.

The Grassroots food philosophy is grounded in a profound commitment to supporting local producers, and over

147

the years they have worked hard to build relationships with farmers and growers province-wide, including Northwood Farm near Hafford, Pine View Farms outside of Saskatoon, and growers Chris and Wanetta Dunlop, who farm near Clavet. The Grassroots approach to sourcing local is unique in that they view the relationships as reciprocal, meaning that while local suppliers grow specific ingredients for them, they also build their menus based on what's available. If a farmer stops by with a surplus load of beets from the season, for instance, Dale will send out an email to all the chefs letting them know that beets are on the menu for the coming weeks. The team also processes an enormous amount of fresh produce during the warmer months by pickling, preserving, dehydrating, and cold storing to extend its life into the winter. Their overall approach is grounded in natural growing cycles and the ability to be creative and flexible with the ingredients they have on hand, encapsulating farm-to-table in a very real sense.

As one of the first restaurants to diversify the collective palate of the city, Ayden was instrumental in pushing forward the province's emerging food scene. Their solid reputation says it all, as the restaurant has been the recipient of much recognition over the years, on both a provincial and national scale. There's always a lively energy to the place, as people gather together for exceptional food and drink, taking in one of the province's most celebrated culinary experiences right in the heart of downtown Saskatoon.

Ayden Kitchen & Bar's
Dill-Cured Diefenbaker Trout with
Beet and Wild Blueberry Condiment

—

>> MAKES 6-8 SNACK SERVINGS
>> TIME: 45 MINUTES + 40 MINUTES-1 HOUR TO CURE
>> GLUTEN-FREE

This elegant and simple dish was created by executive chef Benet Hunt, who notes that Diefenbaker trout is a staple on Ayden's menu—cured, roasted, potted, or raw. Diefenbaker trout comes from Lake Diefenbaker, a popular Saskatchewan fishing destination known for its abundant trout. The vibrantly coloured condiment also features several provincial flavours, including beets and wild blueberries, and has a punchy flavour that pairs well with the delicate flavour of the fish. This dish is a perfect appetizer option for a dinner party. It pairs well with crackers or sourdough bread.

Diefenbaker Trout

12 oz fresh Diefenbaker trout, deboned and skinned*
½ tsp whole caraway seeds
½ tsp whole dill seeds
½ tsp whole black peppercorns
½ cup kosher salt
¼ cup packed brown sugar
¼ cup chopped fresh dill sprigs
2 Tbsp grated lemon zest

Condiment

1 cup grated raw beets
1 cup fresh or frozen wild blueberries**
1 small shallot, diced
½ cup red wine vinegar
¼ cup granulated sugar
2½ Tbsp Worcestershire sauce
1 Tbsp creamed or finely grated horseradish
Sea salt and ground black pepper

Garnish

½ cup sour cream
14-16 small fresh dill sprigs
2 Tbsp finely grated horseradish

DIEFENBAKER TROUT

1. Wash the trout under cold running water and then pat it dry with paper towel. Set it aside on a rimmed baking sheet.
2. Place the caraway seeds, dill seeds, and black peppercorns in a small frying pan, and gently toast them over medium heat until fragrant. Keep a close eye on them, as they can burn quickly. Remove from the heat and then use a mortar and pestle to crush them lightly. (Alternatively, you can put the toasted spices in a food processor or blender and pulse lightly to crush them.)
3. Place the crushed spices in a small bowl with the salt, sugar, dill sprigs, and lemon zest. Stir together to combine.
4. Take half of the spice mix and spread it out evenly on a rimmed baking sheet to roughly the size of the trout. Place the trout on top of the mix and pack the remaining spice mix over and around the trout.
5. Place the trout in the fridge, uncovered, to cure. If you are using the tail end of the trout, cure it for 40 minutes, and if you are using the centre cut or thicker end, cure it for 1 hour.
6. While the fish is curing, prepare the condiment (below).
7. Once the fish is cured, gently wash it under cold running water and pat it dry with paper towel.
8. Slice the trout into thin strips, no thicker than ¼ inch. Arrange the trout on a serving plate and put 1 tsp of the condiment and 1 tsp of sour cream on top of each slice. Garnish each slice with a small sprig of fresh dill and a sprinkle of grated horseradish. Serve immediately.

CONDIMENT

1. Place the beets, the blueberries, shallot, vinegar, sugar, and Worcestershire sauce in a medium saucepan over medium-low heat. Stir to combine and bring the mixture to a simmer. Let the

mixture simmer gently, uncovered and undisturbed, until the liquid has almost evaporated, about 15 minutes.

2. Remove from the heat and transfer to a small blender or food processor. Blend on medium speed until the mixture is fairly smooth (a few lumps are okay). Transfer it to a medium bowl and add the horseradish. Stir to combine and season with salt and pepper to taste.

3. Leftover condiment can be refrigerated in an airtight container for up to 1 week.

*Since the fish is being cured and not fully cooked, it is particularly important to source a good, fresh piece of fish. If you cannot find Diefenbaker trout or another kind of trout, use fresh salmon or Arctic char, and ensure the fish is deboned and skinless.
**Regular fresh or frozen blueberries can be substituted if wild ones are not available.

Sourcing tip: For where to find Diefenbaker trout, see the Sourcing Local Guide (page 284).

Ayden Kitchen & Bar's Pile O' Bones Cocktail

—

> » MAKES 1 COCKTAIL +
>   4 CUPS SASKATOON BERRY
>   SYRUP + 1½ CUPS HONEY
>   GINGER SYRUP
> » TIME: 45 MINUTES +
>   4½ HOURS TO STEEP
> » GLUTEN-FREE (OPTION)

This cocktail is by Ayden's bar manager, Eve Poisson, and features whisky from Last Mountain Distillery in Lumsden and gin from Black Fox Farm & Distillery outside Saskatoon. Infusing the whisky with chamomile gives it a fragrant flavour and scent, while the Saskatoon berry syrup adds balance with a hint of sweetness. The cocktail takes its name from the original Cree name for Regina, *oskana kâ-asastêki*, which translates into English as "where the bones are piled," or "Pile O' Bones," referring to the place where bones were left from a hunt.

Chamomile-Infused Whisky

1 (25 oz/750 mL) bottle of Last Mountain Distillery Whisky*

2 chamomile tea bags, or 5–6 fresh chamomile flowers

Saskatoon Berry Syrup

2 cups fresh or frozen Saskatoon berries

3 cups water

3 cups granulated sugar

Honey Ginger Syrup

6 large (each about 3 inches long) pieces of fresh ginger

1 cup honey

1 cup water

Pile O' Bones Cocktail

1½ oz Chamomile-Infused Whisky

½ oz Black Fox Farm & Distillery Gin #3*

½ oz Amaro Montenegro

1 tsp Saskatoon berry syrup

½ tsp honey ginger syrup

2 dashes traditional aromatic bitters

3–5 ice cubes

3–5 Saskatoon berries, for garnish

CHAMOMILE-INFUSED WHISKY

1. Pour the whisky into a large jug and add the chamomile tea bags. Allow it to steep at room temperature for 30 minutes, stirring occasionally.
2. Pour the whisky through a fine-mesh sieve into another jug to remove the tea bags, and then pour it back into the bottle.

SASKATOON BERRY SYRUP

1. Place the Saskatoon berries and water in a medium saucepan and bring to a boil, uncovered, over medium-high heat. Ensure the berries are completely covered by the water.
2. Turn the heat to low and let the mixture simmer, still uncovered, stirring regularly and gently crushing the berries, until the berries are cooked through and release their juices, about 15 minutes. Skim and remove any foam that rises to the top.
3. Add the sugar and simmer for 5 more minutes on low heat, stirring gently to dissolve the sugar. You can add a bit more sugar to taste, if desired.
4. Strain the syrup through a fine-mesh sieve into a jar or container to remove any pieces of berries.
5. Leftover Saskatoon berry syrup can be refrigerated in an airtight container for up to 2 weeks.

HONEY GINGER SYRUP

1. Peel the ginger and cut each piece into ¼-inch-thick slices. Place them in a small saucepan and add the honey and water. Cover and bring to a boil over high heat.
2. Once boiling, turn the heat down to medium, remove the lid, and simmer for 5 minutes, uncovered, stirring occasionally to dissolve the honey.

3. Remove from the heat and let cool at room temperature. Transfer the syrup to an airtight container and let it steep in the fridge for a minimum of 4 hours, and up to overnight.
4. Strain the syrup through a fine-mesh sieve into an airtight container. Discard the ginger.
5. Leftover honey ginger syrup can be refrigerated in an airtight container for up to 2 weeks.

PILE O' BONES COCKTAIL

1. Place all the cocktail ingredients, except the garnish, in a cocktail shaker. Shake hard until frost begins to form on the outside of the shaker, about 15 seconds.
2. Strain the cocktail into a chilled coupe glass, and add the Saskatoon berries for garnish. You can either add the berries directly to the glass or place them on a skewer. Serve immediately.

*Ayden uses whisky in this cocktail from Last Mountain Distillery in Lumsden and gin from Black Fox Farm & Distillery outside of Saskatoon, but both products can be substituted with a different whisky or gin, if desired. To make this recipe gluten-free, ensure you use gluten-free whisky and gin. You can also make less of the chamomile-infused whisky (rather than a full bottle), to match the total number of cocktails you're making.

Sourcing tip: For where to find Black Fox Farm & Distillery products, Last Mountain Distillery products, and Saskatoon berries, see the Sourcing Local Guide (pages 282, 288, and 291).

2917 Early Drive
Saskatoon, SK S7H 3K5
(306) 249-3287
gudeats.ca

GÜD EATS

As the province's only 100 percent vegan fast food-style restaurant, Güd Eats is reinventing comfort food classics like burgers, tacos, and poutine, using whole-food, plant-based ingredients. It's heaven for anyone who is vegan or has food allergies, and for those new to plant-based food, it's what chef Chris Cole considers a comforting, familiar path to veganism.

With a background in professional cooking, Chris and his partner, Robyn Chatlain, started Güd as a food truck in 2017. Menu staples like Chickn' 'N Waffles and Mac 'N Cheez were wildly popular at local events that year, and, using that traction, they opened Güd's permanent location in Saskatoon that autumn.

Their motto of "crave-worthy plant-based eats" is entirely fitting, as they offer food you can indulge in but feel good about at the same time. Forget about whether or not you like vegan food. If you like food—and I assume you do if you're reading this —you'll like Güd Eats. While that might seem like a bold claim, the menu is built around classic fast food-style eats that most people already know and love. Although Chris and Robyn have been vegan since 2010, Chris admits he loved traditional fast food growing up. With Güd, he wanted to make plant-based eating approachable for everyone.

In addition to the restaurant, Güd is a vegan micro grocer, stocking sweet treats and kitchen staples like dry goods, meat and dairy alternatives, and vegan candy. In 2021 they added their own line of vegan sauces to the roster, including the delicious Dilly Ranch, Chili Mayo, and Caesar Dressing (my personal favourite!). Looking back, Chris says that it's been quite the journey from the early days of the food truck to where they are now, and as awareness of the benefits of plant-based eating grows, he notes that plans for expansion are definitely on the horizon.

Güd Eats' Vegan Green Chili Mac 'N Cheez with Chili Mayo

—

» MAKES 4–6 SERVINGS + ⅔ CUP MAYO
» TIME: 1 HOUR
» GLUTEN-FREE (OPTION) + VEGAN

Vegan Green Chili Mac 'N Cheez

1 cup peeled and medium-diced yellow potato*

½ cup peeled and medium-diced sweet potato

½ cup medium-diced carrot

⅓ cup small-diced yellow onion

2 garlic cloves, chopped

⅔ cup whole raw cashews

8 cups dry macaroni pasta (gluten-free if preferred)

⅓ cup reserved cooking water

⅓ cup nutritional yeast**

¼ cup tapioca starch

2 Tbsp arrowroot powder**

1 Tbsp fine Himalayan pink salt or sea salt

¾ tsp dry mustard powder

A pinch of ground turmeric

A pinch of ground paprika

¼ cup + 3 Tbsp unsweetened oat milk

¼ cup + 2½ Tbsp canned coconut milk***

3 Tbsp vegan butter

1½ Tbsp freshly squeezed lemon juice

1 Tbsp olive oil

1 can (4½ oz/127 mL) of chopped green chilies

Güd's Mac 'N Cheez is so gooey and creamy that you'll have a hard time believing it's vegan. The sauce is rich, tangy, and zesty, while the chili mayo and green chilies add a bit of heat. The cheez sauce is a great staple recipe for any kitchen, and works well on nachos, in dips and casseroles, and, let's be honest, on its own as well. You can use the Mac 'N Cheez as a base recipe and tailor it to your liking by adding sun-dried tomatoes, jalapeños, or even vegan hot dogs.

VEGAN GREEN CHILI MAC 'N CHEEZ

1. Fill a medium pot halfway with water and bring it to a rolling boil over high heat.
2. Once boiling, turn the heat to medium and add the potato, sweet potato, carrot, onion, garlic, and cashews. Partially cover the pot and cook until all the ingredients are extremely soft, 10–15 minutes. Check them with a fork to make sure they are tender all the way through, which will ensure they blend well.
3. Meanwhile, prepare the chili mayo (below). Set it aside in the fridge, uncovered, until you are ready to serve.
4. Cook the macaroni in a large pot of boiling water until al dente, using the timing on the package. Drain and set aside.
5. Remove the vegetables, garlic, and cashews from the water using a slotted spoon, reserving ⅓ cup of the cooking water. Place them in a high-powered blender. (See tip.) Add the reserved cooking water, nutritional yeast, tapioca starch, arrowroot powder, salt, mustard powder, turmeric, paprika, both milks, butter, lemon juice, and oil and blend on high speed until the sauce is creamy and smooth.
6. Place the sauce in the pot you cooked the pasta in and heat it over medium heat, stirring occasionally, until it is almost boiling. Add the cooked pasta and canned green chilies to the sauce, and fold them in gently with a spoon or spatula.
7. Pour into a large casserole dish or divide into individual portions for serving. Top with a scoop of the chili mayo and jalapeño peppers or bread crumbs (if using). Serve immediately.

Chili Mayo

½ cup vegan mayo
2¼ tsp sriracha
2¼ tsp sambal oelek (chili
  garlic sauce)
1 tsp rice vinegar

Optional Garnish

Jalapeño peppers,
  to taste
Dried bread crumbs,
  to taste (gluten-free
  if preferred)

CHILI MAYO

1. Place all the chili mayo ingredients in a small bowl and mix together with a spoon or spatula until well combined.
2. Leftover chili mayo can be refrigerated in an airtight container for up to 1 week.

*If you want to make a truly authentic version of this dish, measure the first four ingredients by weight: yellow potato (5 oz), sweet potato (2 oz), carrot (2 oz), and yellow onion (1½ oz).
**Look for nutritional yeast and arrowroot powder in the bulk or natural section at the grocery store, or at your local organic or bulk foods store.
***Shake up the canned coconut milk prior to opening and measuring it.

Tip: A Vitamix, NutriBullet, or high-powered blender of comparable quality are the only appliances that will work for the vegan cheez sauce. A food processor or immersion blender will not blend the sauce to the correct consistency.

721 Broadway Avenue
Saskatoon, SK S7N 1B3
(306) 665-7991
caloriesrestaurant.ca

CALORIES BAKERY & RESTAURANT

Calories has been a fixture on Broadway Avenue's Smith Block since 1986 and is known for its made-from-scratch menu and strong commitment to sourcing local. The restaurant has become an institution in the province's culinary scene, but it was born out of a simple desire to create a neighbourhood spot where locals could enjoy a genuinely good cup of coffee.

In the 1980s, friends Guy Edlund and Janet Palmer mutually lamented the fact that there was nowhere in Saskatoon to get an espresso or cappuccino. As a result, they opened Calories as a dessert and coffee café, introducing the first espresso machine to the city. They quickly gained a reputation for their decadent desserts, with customers stopping by to marvel at the display case. Within a few months they added a lunch menu with a focus on fresh ingredients, which was met with great enthusiasm. As Calories grew to become a community favourite, Broadway Avenue began to evolve into a central hub for the arts. Calories often hosted musicians or artists who were playing at the Broadway Theatre next door, including Connie Kaldor and k.d. lang.

In 1995, Guy left the business and Rémi and Janis Cousyn joined Janet as co-owners until 2000, when they took over in full. Rémi had apprenticed at the Moulin de Mougins in France, and he brought with him a love of French cuisine and an appreciation for a seasonal menu. He expanded the lunch and dinner menus and built relationships with local suppliers. His focus on using regional ingredients to give fresh and simple French dishes a modern twist still forms the heart of the menu today.

Rémi continued to build on Calories' legacy of quality food and service for nearly two decades, until 2019, when current owners Taszia and Karan Thakur bought the business after years in the hospitality industry. Taszia is from Tisdale and attended the Culinary Institute of Canada before travelling and working abroad. In 2013, while doing research for a business plan, she cold-called Rémi in hopes of asking him some questions. After chatting, Rémi told her to give him a call if she ever came back to Saskatchewan. In 2014, Taszia moved to Saskatoon, and, true to his word, Rémi hired her as a cook, then sous chef, and then head chef. As owners, Taszia and Karan are passionate about continuing to work with local farmers and suppliers, and they do plenty of canning, drying, and preserving, ensuring customers can enjoy Saskatchewan ingredients year-round.

The interior of Calories epitomizes old world charm, with original hardwood floors from 1912 and a gorgeous wood bar and pass-through kitchen, which were added during a renovation in 1998. The restaurant's walls feature local art that changes monthly, an initiative that Janet started in the 1990s which continues to this day. Several menu items from the early days are still offered today too, including wild rice bread, toffee cheesecake, and the shmoo torte. They even used to sell T-shirts in the 1990s with "Sorry we're out of Shmoo" on the front and "No, there's none in the back either" on the back. It's traditions like these that give the restaurant a longevity that's rare, rooted in a long-standing history of quality and excellence. To many, Calories will always be a familiar place where you can sink into one of the coveted window seats, cozy up with a glass of wine, and watch the bustling traffic of Broadway Avenue pass you by.

The outside of the Smith Block in October of 1990, showing Calories on the left. The sign reads "Calories: Desserts & Cappuccino."

Calories' Wild Rice Risotto with Fiddleheads and Morels

—

» MAKES 4 SERVINGS
» TIME: 2 HOURS 15 MINUTES
» GLUTEN-FREE

⅔ cup uncooked wild rice

12 cups water, divided

1 Tbsp + 1 tsp salt, divided

2 cups fresh fiddleheads, long ends trimmed or 1 bunch of asparagus, cut into 2-inch pieces

Ice cubes

5 cups low-sodium vegetable stock or broth

2 Tbsp olive oil

6 Tbsp unsalted butter, divided

1 large yellow onion, diced small and divided

3 garlic cloves, minced and divided

1 cup uncooked arborio rice

1 sprig of fresh rosemary or thyme

¼ tsp ground black pepper

½ cup white wine

2 Tbsp finely chopped fresh chives

1 tsp finely chopped fresh tarragon

¼ tsp grated lemon zest

1½ cups fresh whole morel mushrooms*

⅓ cup chèvre

Wild rice risotto is a feature dish at Calories. They use traditional arborio rice for the risotto and add ingredients grown in the province for local flair, including wild rice, morel mushrooms, and fiddleheads. The risotto is creamy, light, and classy, and is meant to be enjoyed alongside a glass of chilled rosé or pinot noir, or a refreshing spritzer. Taszia notes this dish features spring ingredients from Saskatchewan, but that the risotto can be used as a base and modified for any season. Try chanterelle mushrooms in summer, butternut squash and candied pecans in fall, or lentils and roasted beets in winter.

1. Place the wild rice, 4 cups of the water, and a pinch of salt in a medium-sized pot. Bring it to a boil over high heat, and then turn down the heat to medium and simmer, uncovered, until the rice just begins to split open, about 1 hour. Drain the rice and set it aside.

2. Add the remaining 8 cups of water and the 1 Tbsp of salt to a large pot and bring it to a boil over high heat. Add the fiddleheads and then turn the heat to medium-high and let them boil until tender, 8–10 minutes. Fiddleheads should not be eaten raw, so ensure they are fully cooked. Drain the fiddleheads and put them in a large bowl of ice to shock them and stop the cooking process. Once they are cold, drain them and lay them on a towel-lined plate to remove the excess water. (Alternatively, if you are substituting asparagus for the fiddleheads, blanch the asparagus in water for 2–3 minutes in a medium saucepan over medium-high heat, and then strain and shock the asparagus on ice.)

3. Place the stock in a large pot and bring to a simmer on low heat, to keep it warm while you're preparing the risotto.

4. In another large pot over medium-high heat, place the oil and 2 Tbsp of the butter. Add ⅔ of the onions and sauté until they begin to caramelize, about 10 minutes. Add ⅔ of the garlic and cook to combine with the other ingredients for about 1 minute. Add the arborio rice and stir to coat all of the grains with the fat in the pot. Add the 1 tsp salt, the rosemary sprig, and pepper.

5. Add the wine and turn the heat to medium. Reduce the mixture until almost all the wine is gone. Add about 1 cup of the warm vegetable stock to the pot, and stir constantly until almost all of the stock has been absorbed by the rice.

6. Continue to add the stock about 1 cup at a time, stirring regularly, until the liquid has evaporated and the rice is almost cooked, about 20 minutes. Set aside ¼ cup of the stock. Stir in the cooked wild rice, 2 Tbsp of the butter, the chives, tarragon, and lemon zest.

7. Place the remaining 2 Tbsp of butter in a frying pan over medium-high heat and sauté the morels until they begin to brown, about 5 minutes. Add the remaining onions and sauté for 5 more minutes. Add the cooked fiddleheads, and sauté until heated through, 1–2 minutes. Stir in the remaining garlic and sauté for 1 more minute. Season to taste with salt and pepper, if needed.
8. Remove the sprig of rosemary from the pot. If needed, add the remaining ¼ cup of stock to adjust the consistency of the risotto. It should be creamy, but not too thick or runny.
9. Divide the risotto between four individual serving bowls. Divide the fiddleheads and morels evenly between each portion, and scatter the chèvre on top. Serve immediately.

*Morel mushrooms can be substituted with whole chanterelle mushrooms or cremini or button mushrooms, cut into quarters.

Sourcing tip: For where to find fiddleheads and morel and chanterelle mushrooms, see the Sourcing Local Guide (pages 286 and 288).

Regina

—

Traditions surrounding food are often a source of communal and personal identity, as well as a way to share culture and connection with others. This chapter features many chefs and business owners who are preserving such traditions and building on them, taking recipes they grew up with and recreating them on the Prairies. Many of the recipes feature dishes that have been crafted with authenticity in mind, showcasing flavours from around the world that have likewise made their mark on the provincial culinary scene.

Food is the main way that my family celebrates our cultural identity, and while other cultural traditions have been forgotten over the years, those surrounding food have endured. Most of my great-grandparents immigrated to Canada from Ukraine, Poland, and Hungary between 1900 and 1930, and they brought with them many treasured recipes. Staples included classics like perogies, cabbage rolls, borscht, and pickled herring, not to mention Hungarian chicken paprikash, nalysnyky (a Ukrainian crepe stuffed with cottage cheese), poppyseed rolls and cakes, and beet leaf rolls (buns baked with beet leaves, dill, and cream).

Some of these food traditions have been passed down to me and my sister, Aunya. Perogies are one such item, and come holidays or gatherings there are always plenty to go around. The classic potato perogies are my favourite, but my baba has also made sauerkraut, prune, and blueberry perogies in the past. Several years ago, Aunya and I received our first formal lesson in perogy-making from my mom, who thought it was time we learned how this family favourite was made. Since then, Aunya and I have taken the liberty of forming our own traditions around perogies. Every year at Christmas we make what we've termed "the massive perogy," which is an enormous potato and dough creation made from leftover perogy filling and dough scraps. The massive perogy is almost impossible to cook, but still we try, awkwardly manoeuvring it around in boiling water so it doesn't fall apart. Speaking from experience, if you end up getting stuck with the massive perogy come dinnertime, chances are you won't have room for much else.

Other family staples that we still make today include red beet borscht, cabbage rolls, and Ukrainian Easter bread, also known as babka. As a child, I remember being enamoured with Easter bread, the round loaves shiny and golden on the outside, soft and fluffy on the inside. In the weeks that followed Easter, I'd devour huge slabs of the bread, slathered in jam or melted butter. It was almost painful having to wait until the next year for this traditional treat to come around again. Similarly, my husband's mom's side of the family is proudly Swedish, and whenever his grandma and mom make palt (a meat-filled potato dumpling) or lefse (a flatbread with Norwegian origins), his family is ecstatic and cannot get their hands on them fast enough.

In many of the interviews I conducted for this chapter, chefs and business owners spoke about how they were recreating food staples from their childhood or family culture and using those dishes to educate customers about authentic cuisines. Their approach has certainly struck a chord, as many establishments have found a lasting place within Regina's community. Sometimes, when you take the first few bites of a meal or a certain dish, you can just tell that the flavour has been years in the making, perfected over time by generations past. In many ways, food is one of the simplest and most direct communication tools we have, something we can use to reconnect with our roots and share what is authentic about who we are and where we come from.

1611 Victoria Avenue
Regina, SK S4P 0P8
(306) 757-6733
italianstardeli.com

ITALIAN STAR DELI

Italian Star Deli is a bustling place, buzzing with energy and lively chatter. When you walk in, aisles of neat grocery shelves with products imported from all over Europe lead you to the main event: the deli counter. The Italian flag hangs proudly overhead as staff busy themselves wrapping up specialty meats, cutting generous slices of delicious, fragrant cheeses, and preparing the deli's legendary paninis for the lunch rush.

On the day of our interview, I'm greeted by Carlo Giambattista, who is the second generation of the Giambattista family to run the deli. Known by locals for his friendly banter and wide smile, he hands me a steaming cup of coffee— and with a wink mentions that he added an extra shot of espresso. He says that people love the deli for its atmosphere, and it's easy to see why: the environment is warm, welcoming, and energetic; jokes fly back and forth between family members; and regulars are called by name and handed their usual order.

It's safe to say that Italian Star Deli is a bit of an institution in Regina. Carlo's parents, Frank and Gina Giambattista, immigrated to Regina in 1957 and 1958,

respectively, from Molise, Italy. In 1966 they bought Italian Star Deli, at that time a small confectionary business. They decided to keep the name, but instead of continuing to run it as a confectionary, they aimed to respond to the growing demand for Italian food products in the city. Carlo illustrates the difficulty in finding staple items at the time with a story about how his mother used to purchase cans of pork and beans and then wash them off with water, just to get the red kidney beans she needed to make a traditional fagioli soup.

Frank later took a job with the City of Regina and Gina poured her heart into Italian Star Deli, building a reputation based on passion and hospitality. In 1979, Carlo joined his mother full-time and expanded the deli side of the business, introducing staples like their panini, which feature Mama Gina's special marinade spread. The operation is truly a family affair, as Carlo's children, Marina and Gino, are now involved in the business. Marina works as a hands-on deli specialist and Gino can often be found chatting up customers as he rings them through the till. Today the deli offers

The mural on the side of the building at Italian Star Deli shows Frank and Gina Giambattista's 1956 wedding photo, right before they immigrated to Canada. It was painted by Saskatchewan-based graffiti artist David Loran.

catering too, with favourites like cannoli, meat and cheese trays, and house-made bruschetta.

As homage to Frank and Gina, Carlo commissioned Saskatchewan-based graffiti artist David Loran to paint a mural of his parents' 1956 wedding photo on the side of the building. The mural has become iconic in Regina, much like the deli itself. Visits from the Saskatchewan Roughriders and local celebrities are common, and for years Carlo kept up a tradition of posting photographs with notable customers on the deli's walls. Although they have done some renovations over the years, much of the original layout from 1927 remains the same today.

With a legacy of 56 years and counting, Italian Star Deli is certainly a place worth visiting, not only for their famous deli eats but also to experience the heart and soul of the Giambattista family in action.

Italian Star Deli's Gourmet Sicilian Cannoli

—

» MAKES 30 CANNOLI
» TIME: 1 HOUR 15 MINUTES

Filling

2 cups ricotta cheese
2 cups mascarpone cheese
½ cup icing sugar
⅓ cup chopped raw unsalted pistachios
⅓ cup mini chocolate chips, milk or dark
2 Tbsp mixed candied fruit
1 tsp orange blossom water
½ tsp ground cinnamon

Shells

1 cup regular milk chocolate chips
30 cannoli shells
1 cup regular dark chocolate chips

Garnish

⅓ cup mini chocolate chips, milk or dark
30 whole raw unsalted pistachios

This recipe for gourmet Sicilian cannoli was handed down to Gina, and then adapted by Carlo's wife, Heather. The Giambattista recipe is slightly different than a traditional cannoli, because it contains mascarpone cheese, which gives it a very rich, almost cream cheese flavour. The cannoli filling is light and fluffy, and features a subtle hint of pistachio and a touch of sweetness from the candied fruit. Adding chocolate to the inside of the shells keeps the cannoli fresh and provides a delightfully satisfying crunch. Carlo recommends pairing cannoli with chilled limoncello or something bubbly, like Prosecco or an asti.

FILLING

1. Place all the cannoli filling ingredients in a medium bowl. Using a handheld electric mixer, beat on medium speed until well combined. Cover the bowl with plastic wrap and refrigerate.

SHELLS

1. Melt the regular milk chocolate chips in a small bowl in the microwave for 15-second intervals, stirring between each interval until completely melted. Using an offset spatula or a small spoon, spread a thin layer of melted milk chocolate on the inside of each cannoli shell. Place the finished shells on a rimmed baking sheet.
2. Melt the regular dark chocolate chips in a small bowl in the microwave for 15-second intervals, stirring between each interval until completely melted. Dip both ends of each cannoli shell into the melted dark chocolate. Place the finished shells back on the baking sheet and then refrigerate until the chocolate is firm and dry, 5–10 minutes.

GARNISH AND ASSEMBLY

1. Remove the cannoli filling and shells from the fridge. Fill a pastry piping bag with the filling, and then pipe some into each cannoli shell. They should be full from one end to the other. You will need to fill the pastry piping bag multiple times to use up all the filling. Place the completed cannoli back onto the rimmed baking sheet. (Alternatively, if you do not have a pastry piping bag, you can use a large resealable plastic bag. Make a small hole by cutting off one of the bottom corners of the bag on the diagonal, and then fill the bag with the cannoli filling and pipe it into the shells.)

2. Put the mini chocolate chips for garnish in a small bowl. To garnish, dip one end of each piped cannoli shell into the mini chocolate chips and place 1 whole pistachio on the other end of each shell. Repeat with the rest of the cannoli and then serve immediately.

Sourcing tip: For where to find cannoli shells, see the Sourcing Local Guide (page 282).

2903 Powerhouse Drive
Regina, SK S4N 0A1
(306) 352-7593
skyecafeandbistro.com

SKYE CAFÉ & BISTRO

Skye Café & Bistro is a calming space reminiscent of an atrium, with soft sunlight streaming in and plants decorating the restaurant in all shades of green. Owned by husband-and-wife duo Milton Rebello and Louise Lu, Skye is named after their oldest daughter and housed in the Saskatchewan Science Centre along Wascana Lake.

The couple opened the restaurant in 2016 after spending years in the hospitality industry. Originally from India, Milton is a Red Seal chef and has worked in kitchens from Kenya to Qatar to New York. After moving to Canada, he worked at the Fairmont Chateau Lake Louise and jumped around the hotel scene before landing at Regina's Hotel Saskatchewan. He's also an avid culinary competitor: he came in first at Gold Medal Plates Regina 2012 and won a medal at the 2013 Canadian Culinary Championships.

Louise is from China and studied professional cooking at the Northern Alberta Institute of Technology (NAIT) in Edmonton. She is the executive chef at Skye and has a talent for both culinary and visual arts. The restaurant's windows feature her delicate, hand-painted designs and warm drinks are served in her handmade clay mugs, which provide a creative touch.

The artistry extends to the menu, which focuses on marrying Prairie ingredients with the flavours of Louise and Milton's travels, including dishes like beef ramen, shakshuka, and masti (Mumbai street food). They are also the exclusive caterer for the Science Centre, and host monthly dinners and private events. Central to all their endeavours is a commitment to sustainability—they have an on-site garden and compost their food scraps—and a focus on cooking with organic, seasonal ingredients. There's a deep thoughtfulness to everything they do, and while they offer an unforgettable culinary experience, Milton says that at its core, Skye is "a happy place," simply an extension of their travels and home.

Skye's Mediterranean Bowl

—

» MAKES 5–6 SERVINGS
» TIME: 1 HOUR 30 MINUTES + OVERNIGHT
  TO SOAK + 2 HOURS TO CHILL
» GLUTEN-FREE + VEGAN

Lentil and Chickpea Falafel

1½ cups dried chickpeas
¼ cup dried brown lentils
¼ cup dried green lentils
½ large yellow onion, diced small
6 garlic cloves, minced
2 Tbsp finely chopped fresh parsley
2 Tbsp finely chopped fresh cilantro
1 tsp ground cumin
1 tsp sea salt
1 tsp crushed red pepper flakes
2 Tbsp tahini
6 Tbsp chickpea flour
Vegetable oil, for deep frying

Beet Hummus

1 medium-sized beet
1½ cups cooked chickpeas (drained
    and rinsed if using canned)
2 garlic cloves, minced
2 Tbsp tahini
½ tsp sea salt
½ tsp ground cumin
2 Tbsp freshly squeezed lemon juice
3 Tbsp extra-virgin olive oil

Salad*

2 heads of lettuce, washed and chopped
2 cups chopped vegetables, your choice
    (Skye uses cucumber, radish, and
    tomato)
Salad toppers, your choice (Skye uses
    pickled radish, olives, feta, and crispy
    chickpeas)
Balsamic vinaigrette, to taste**
Pita bread, for serving (use gluten-free
    if preferred)

This Mediterranean bowl has been on Skye's menu since it first opened, and it remains one of their most popular items. It's a healthy, earthy, colourful dish with fresh, crunchy vegetables and a creamy, pink beet hummus. The bowl showcases local ingredients and uses in-house pickled radish, and beets from Milton and Louise's garden. The crispy Lebanese-style falafel is made with Saskatchewan lentils and chickpeas and has a deliciously complex spice palate. The team at Skye makes hundreds of falafel every week, as the Mediterranean bowl is also on their catering menu and they sell falafel to go by the dozen. Note that the lentils and chickpeas need to soak overnight.

LENTIL AND CHICKPEA FALAFEL

1. Place the chickpeas and both types of lentils in a large bowl with enough cold water to cover them by at least 2 inches. Let them soak overnight, uncovered, on the counter. The next day, drain them when you are ready to start the recipe.
2. Place the soaked chickpeas and lentils in a food processor fitted with the steel blade. Add the onion, garlic, parsley, cilantro, cumin, salt, and red pepper flakes. Process on medium speed until blended, but not puréed.
3. Add the tahini and process again until well combined.
4. Add the chickpea flour and process again. The dough should form a small ball in the food processor and no longer stick to your hands when you touch it. If needed, add a little bit more chickpea flour, about 1 tsp at a time, until the desired consistency is reached.
5. Transfer the falafel dough to an airtight container and refrigerate it for 2 hours. Refrigerating the falafel helps it to hold together during cooking.
6. Meanwhile prepare the beet hummus (below).
7. Once the falafel is done chilling, remove it from the fridge. Using clean hands, form the falafel into medium-sized balls, each about the size of a large walnut. Place the completed falafel balls on a rimmed baking sheet lined with parchment paper.

8. In a large, deep, heavy-bottomed pot, heat 3 inches of vegetable oil (canola works well) over medium-high heat until it reaches a temperature of 375°F (190°C). The oil should not come up more than halfway along the side of the pot. Check the temperature with an instant-read thermometer to ensure consistent frying heat. (Alternatively, if you have a deep fryer you can use that to fry the falafel. Follow the instructions for your brand of deep fryer.)

9. Using a slotted spoon, carefully lower one of the falafel balls into the pot as a deep-fry test. It should hold together and become crispy. If it falls apart, you may need to add a little bit more chickpea flour to the remaining balls and then test it again.

10. Carefully lower 6–8 falafel balls into the pot using a slotted spoon, and fry until crispy and golden brown, 3–5 minutes on each side. Remove them from the pot with the slotted spoon and allow them to cool and drain on a plate lined with paper towel.

11. Repeat with the remaining falafel, ensuring the temperature of the oil remains consistent at 375°F (190°C) throughout. You may have to let it return to temperature between batches.

12. Set the falafel aside until you are ready to serve. To keep them warm, place them in the oven at its very lowest setting on a baking sheet for up to 15 minutes.

BEET HUMMUS

1. Place the beet in a medium pot with enough water to cover it. Bring to a boil on high heat, turn the heat down to medium-high, and let it boil until soft and cooked through, about 25 minutes.

2. Using tongs, remove the beet from the water and let it cool enough to touch. Remove the skin and then chop the beet into small chunks. Place the chunks in a blender or food processor fitted with the steel blade and purée until smooth. Measure out 2 Tbsp of the purée for the hummus, and set the rest aside.

3. Place the 2 Tbsp of purée and the chickpeas, garlic, tahini, salt, cumin, and lemon juice in the blender or food processor. Blend on low speed while gradually adding the oil through the spout or opening at the top. Continue to blend on low speed until the mixture becomes a smooth paste. For a stronger beet flavour, you can add a little bit more of the beet purée, 1 tsp at a time, to taste.

4. Set the beet hummus aside in the fridge, covered, until you are ready to serve.

SALAD AND ASSEMBLY

1. Take an individual salad bowl and, using a spoon or spatula, spread a generous helping of the beet hummus along one half of the bowl.

2. Add the lettuce, chopped vegetables, and salad toppers to the bowl.

3. Add 2–3 lentil and chickpea falafels and drizzle some balsamic vinaigrette over the salad. Repeat the process with the remaining servings. Serve immediately with pita bread.

*The salad portion of the bowl can be changed up to include whatever vegetables and toppings you prefer. Note that if you are making this recipe vegan, do not use feta as a salad topper.

**Instead of balsamic vinaigrette, use any type of dressing you want for the salad. Alternatively, you can use the beet hummus as a dressing or substitute extra-virgin olive oil for the dressing.

MALINCHE

Mariana Brito was born in Mexico City and raised in Tijuana, Mexico. As Malinche's founder, she has a passion for using food as a tool to educate people about Mexican culture.

After attending culinary school in Mexico, Mariana travelled and worked in restaurants before moving to Saskatchewan in 2010. In 2015, she started a pop-up restaurant in Regina with her former partner, Kieran Lee LeMoal, which they called The Backyard. Kieran is an avid gardener, and together they created tasting menus using Prairie ingredients. Incorporating that same local approach, Mariana and Kieran opened Malinche in 2016, first as a pop-up restaurant and then as a stationary food truck at Malty National Brewing. In 2019, Malinche moved to Pile O' Bones Brewing Company, where they offered a taproom menu with favourites like tacos and tostadas. For the five years that they ran the business, they also had a restaurant garden and an extensive preserving program, ensuring Saskatchewan produce appeared on the menu even in winter.

Malinche takes its name from La Malinche, a multilingual Indigenous woman who was enslaved in 1519 during the Spanish conquest of the Aztec Empire. As an interpreter for the Spanish conquistador Hernán Cortés, La Malinche was very much a bridge between two worlds. For Mariana, the name represents the experience of translating Mexican culture on the Prairies and, in this case, communicating through food. She built the menu around the culinary traditions she grew up with, combining Prairie ingredients with bold, authentic Mexican flavours.

Mariana says that being part of a community where businesses support each other's growth has been an incredible experience, and she's grateful for the connections she's made in Regina. After a decade in Saskatchewan, in 2021 she decided to move back to Mexico and reconnect with her roots, and at time of writing, Malinche was in the process of finding a new owner and location. For the latest updates on this Regina favourite, stay tuned to their website and social media.

Malinche's Salsa Verde and Salsa Roja

—

Salsa verde and salsa roja are two of Mariana's staple recipes, and can be served alongside dishes like burritos, chimichangas, and enchiladas. Both recipes feature similar ingredients—garlic, onion, and árbol chili peppers—but the way the ingredients are used in each recipe lends each one a different taste. The salsa roja has a slightly sweeter flavour, while the salsa verde is more acidic. Both recipes are best prepared when tomatoes and tomatillos are in season, but they can be canned to prolong their shelf life.

» MAKES 5 CUPS
» TIME: 45 MINUTES
» GLUTEN-FREE + VEGAN

15 medium-sized tomatillos, husks removed*
½ medium white onion
1 unpeeled garlic clove
¼ cup grapeseed or avocado oil
1 árbol chili pepper, stem removed
½ cup pickled jalapeño peppers
10 sprigs of fresh cilantro, chopped
1 Tbsp sea salt
1½ tsp ground black pepper

SALSA VERDE

1. Place the whole tomatillos in a large pot with enough water to cover them completely. Ensure that there are at least 3 inches between where the water ends and the top of the pot, so that it does not boil over. Bring to a boil over high heat, turn the heat down to medium-high, and cook the tomatillos until soft but not falling apart, about 10 minutes. The tomatillos should change from bright green to a dull, darker green. Once cooked, drain and set aside.

2. Cut the onion half into quarters. Place the onion and garlic in a small frying pan over medium heat to dry-roast them. Cover the frying pan with a lid to allow the onion and garlic to sweat. Let them roast for a total of 15 minutes, at about 5 minutes per side, to ensure all sides are evenly roasted. The process of dry roasting will soften and slightly char the onion and garlic, and the garlic is left unpeeled so that it does not burn. Once they're soft and slightly charred on all sides, remove the pan from the heat to let it cool, and peel the garlic once it is cool enough to touch.

3. Heat the oil in a small frying pan over medium heat. Add the árbol chili pepper and lightly fry for 3–5 minutes. Watch carefully so that it does not burn. Remove the pepper from the pan using tongs or a slotted spoon and set aside. Remove the pan from the heat and set it aside to save the oil (you can keep it in the pan) for later in the recipe.

4. Place the cooked tomatillos, dry-roasted onion and garlic, fried chili pepper, jalapeños, cilantro, salt, and pepper in a high-powered blender. Blend on high speed until the mixture is smooth and well combined.

5. Pour the oil from the frying pan into a medium pot (large enough to fit all of the salsa), and warm it over medium heat. Add the blended salsa, turn up the heat to high, and bring it to a boil. Turn the heat down to medium-low and let the salsa simmer, uncovered, stirring occasionally, 10–15 minutes.

6. Remove the salsa from the heat and let cool at room temperature. Add a bit more salt to taste, if desired. The salsa can be canned to

extend its shelf life, or stored in an airtight container in the fridge for up to 1 week.

*The size of tomatillos can vary, but their total weight should be just under 3½ lb (1.5 kg).

SALSA ROJA

» MAKES 5 CUPS
» TIME: 45 MINUTES
» GLUTEN-FREE + VEGAN

15 medium-sized Roma tomatoes*

1 árbol chili pepper, stem removed

1 medium white onion, cut in quarters

6 peeled garlic cloves

10 sprigs fresh cilantro, chopped

1 Tbsp sea salt

1½ tsp ground black pepper

¼ cup grapeseed or avocado oil

1. Place the tomatoes in a medium pot with enough water to cover them. Ensure that there are at least 3 inches between where the water ends and the top of the pot so that it does not boil over. Bring to a boil over high heat, turn the heat down to medium-high, and cook the tomatoes until soft but not falling apart, about 10 minutes. Once cooked, drain and set them aside.
2. Place the chili pepper in a small frying pan over medium heat to dry-roast it. Let it roast for a total of 5 minutes, uncovered, at about 2–3 minutes per side, to ensure both sides are evenly charred. Be careful that it does not burn. Remove from the heat and set aside.
3. Place the cooked tomatoes, dry-roasted chili pepper, onion, garlic, cilantro, salt, and pepper in a high-powered blender. Blend on high speed until the mixture is smooth and well combined.
4. Place the oil in a medium pot (large enough to fit all of the salsa) and warm it over medium heat. Add the blended salsa, turn up the heat to high, and bring to a boil. Turn down the heat to medium-low and let the salsa simmer, uncovered, stirring occasionally, 10–15 minutes.
5. Remove the salsa from the heat and let cool at room temperature. Add a bit more salt to taste, if desired. The salsa can be canned to extend its shelf life, or stored in an airtight container in the fridge for up to 1 week.

*The size of Roma tomatoes can vary, but their total weight should be just under 3½ lb (1.5 kg).

Tip: A Vitamix or high-powered blender of comparable quality are the only appliances that will work for these recipes. A food processor, lower-quality blender, or immersion blender will not blend the salsas to the correct smooth consistency.

Sourcing tip: For where to find árbol chili peppers and tomatillos, see the Sourcing Local Guide (page 278).

2234 14th Avenue
Regina, SK S4P 0X8
(306) 522-3500
tangerineregina.ca

TANGERINE: THE FOOD BAR

Aimee Schulhauser chose to name her restaurant Tangerine after one of her favourite Led Zeppelin songs, and because it sounded fresh and energetic. It's certainly fitting, as Tangerine: The Food Bar is a bright space with plenty of natural light and a cheerful, lively energy. The front counter is always well-stocked with baked goods, including gluten-free and vegan options. A chalkboard menu, which changes weekly based on what's in season, runs along the back wall.

Aimee fell in love with cooking when she was in university, after realizing she had no idea how to cook. She bought a few food magazines to teach herself the basics and stumbled upon a new passion. She later attended the Southern Alberta Institute of Technology (SAIT) in Calgary and obtained a Professional Cooking Diploma. In 2005 she moved back to Regina to start her first business, Evolution Catering and Fine Foods, followed by Tangerine in 2010.

While she was running her business, she began offering cooking classes out of Tangerine's kitchen. The classes were met with overwhelming interest, with customers lining up at 6 AM to sign up. As a result, in 2014 she renovated Tangerine's basement and opened Schoolhaus Culinary Arts, which now offers private and public classes on everything from cake decorating and Italian cuisine to building confidence in the kitchen.

Tangerine has grown to include Meetings by Tangerine, catering services, and Slice Café, which opened in 2020 near Wascana Park. Aimee is also a past recipient of a YWCA Regina Women of Distinction Award and a Saskatchewan Chamber of Commerce ABEX Award. Her food philosophy is rooted in the belief that there's a chef in all of us, and she describes Tangerine as a "culinary playground," where a dash of creativity can always lead to something new.

Tangerine's Quinoa Salad with Lemon Dill Yogurt Dressing

—

» MAKES 3–4 SERVINGS
» TIME: 40 MINUTES
» GLUTEN-FREE

Dressing

½ cup plain yogurt
¼ cup chopped fresh dill
1 Tbsp canola or olive oil
1 Tbsp freshly squeezed
    lemon juice
1 tsp grated lemon zest

Salad

1 cup uncooked quinoa,
    rinsed and drained
2 cups water
1 cup packed spinach
1 green onion, finely sliced
½ cup sweetened dried
    cranberries
¼ cup sliced unsalted
    almonds
½ tsp sea salt

This quinoa salad is Tangerine's most popular salad, and it has been on the menu since Aimee's early days in the catering business. It's a simple, healthy, and filling recipe, with hearty quinoa, crunchy almonds, fresh dill, and a touch of sweetness from the cranberries. Aimee notes that you can modify the salad by bulking it up with more spinach, or adding grilled chicken or tofu for extra protein. It's a perfect option for meal prepping or serving at a gathering or barbeque, and it pairs well with lunch fare like soups, sandwiches, or quiche.

DRESSING

1. Place all the dressing ingredients in a small bowl and stir together to combine. Refrigerate while you prepare the salad.

SALAD

1. Place the quinoa and water in a medium saucepan over medium-high heat and bring to a boil, uncovered. Once boiling, turn the heat to medium and simmer until the quinoa has absorbed all the water, about 10 minutes.
2. Remove from the heat, cover, and let the quinoa steam for 5 minutes. Spread the quinoa out on a rimmed baking sheet to cool, or rinse it under cold water, and set it aside.
3. Chiffonade the spinach by stacking a small handful of spinach leaves in a neat pile. Roll the stack lengthwise into a compact cigar shape, and then slice the spinach into ribbons. Place the chiffonade spinach in a large bowl.
4. Add the cooked quinoa, green onion, cranberries, almonds, and salt. Pour the dressing overtop of the salad, and gently toss until well combined. Add more salt to taste, if needed. Serve immediately.

Tip: If you make this recipe in advance, add everything except for the spinach to avoid wilting. When ready to serve, add the spinach and then mix together to combine.

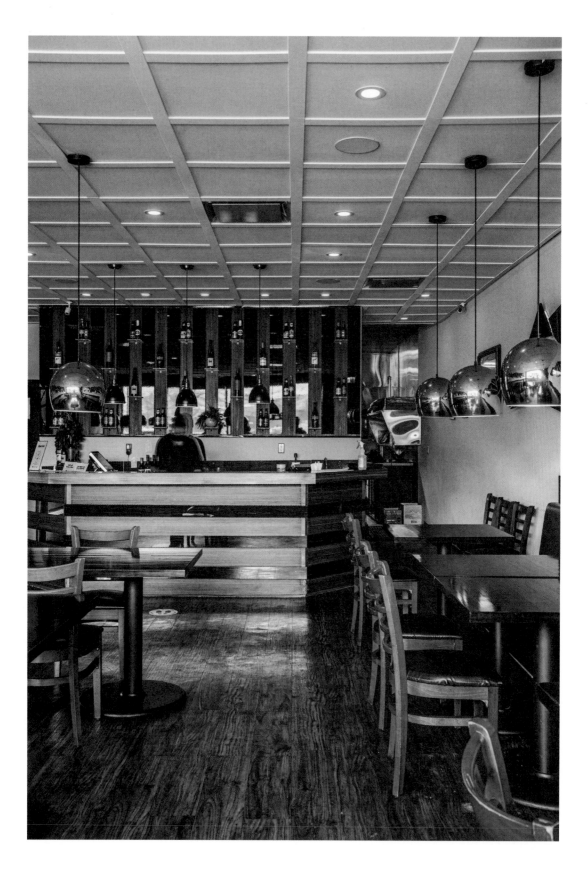

1625 Broad Street
Regina, SK S4P 1X3
(306) 522-4243
+ multiple SK locations
carawaygrill.com

CARAWAY GRILL

Caraway Grill, which serves authentic North Indian cuisine, is one of Regina's best-loved restaurants. Owner Parveen Singh prides himself on providing high-quality food and service and is passionate about crafting dishes that are not only creative, but also incorporate traditional cooking methods.

Originally from northern India, Parveen started his career in restaurants in the New Delhi area, including at Taj Hotels. After living and working in Germany for a while, he moved to Canada in 2005 and opened his first restaurant, Apalla Indian Cuisine, in Toronto in 2008. In 2013, he moved to Regina and opened Caraway, and has since made a name for himself, even competing at Gold Medal Plates Regina in 2016.

The interior of Caraway Grill has a sophisticated feel, with orange, gold, and bronze tones adding a refined warmth. The décor incorporates natural wood and metallic textures, which reflect a glint of light whenever the sun shines into the restaurant. Bronze bowl lights hang above the tables, and a large silver bar stands boldly at one end of the restaurant, where staff can be found filling orders and making drinks.

Caraway Grill is popular for both dine-in and takeout, and in 2021 they expanded with a second Regina location and catering services, as well as their first ever Saskatoon location. Throughout all their endeavours and all the changes, one constant has been their commitment to authenticity and excellence. All of Caraway's dishes are based on Parveen's own recipes, and many menu items like their Indian breads (they have 9 kinds), are cooked in a clay oven, which is a traditional method that creates a smokey, earthy taste. With a focus on flavours true to their roots, Caraway Grill offers a genuine taste of North Indian cuisine right in the heart of the Queen City.

Caraway Grill's Butter Chicken

—

>> MAKES 2 SERVINGS
>> TIME: 45 MINUTES +
   4 HOURS TO MARINATE
>> GLUTEN-FREE (OPTION)

Butter chicken is Caraway Grill's signature dish and is popular with locals and visitors alike. At Caraway Grill, the chicken is cooked in a traditional clay oven for several hours, which results in a slightly smokey flavour, but for this at-home version the chicken can be done in your oven. The butter chicken sauce is creamy and nutty from the cashews and has a mild spice palate. Pair butter chicken with an Indian beer or a glass of wine, plus your favourite rice or warmed naan, which is perfect for dipping in the sauce.

Chicken and Marinade

14 oz boneless chicken
   breast (about 2 large or
   3 small chicken breasts)
1½ tsp freshly squeezed
   lemon juice
1 tsp vegetable oil
¼ tsp red chili powder*
¼ tsp sea salt

Butter Chicken Sauce

1½ cups water
⅓ cup whole unsalted
   cashews
2 firm medium Roma
   tomatoes, diced
   medium**
1 tsp vegetable oil
½ tsp green chili paste*
¼ tsp red chili powder*
¼ tsp sea salt
½ tsp unsalted butter
1 tsp ginger paste
1 tsp garlic paste
2 tsp sweet paprika
½ cup half-and-half
   (10%) cream
1 tsp garam masala*
½ tsp kasoori methi (dried
   fenugreek)*

For serving

Rice or naan (use rice for
   gluten-free version)

CHICKEN AND MARINADE

1. Place the chicken breasts in a medium bowl. Mix together the marinade ingredients and rub the marinade over the chicken. Cover the bowl tightly with plastic wrap and marinate in the fridge for 4 hours.
2. Once the chicken is done marinating, preheat the oven to 400°F (200°C). Lightly grease a medium-sized baking dish or pan with cooking spray and place the marinated chicken breasts in it.
3. Bake the chicken until it reaches an internal temperature of 165°F (74°C), 20–25 minutes.

BUTTER CHICKEN SAUCE

1. Place the water, cashews, tomatoes, oil, chili paste, chili powder, and salt in a medium saucepan over high heat. Mix everything together, cover the pot, and bring to a boil. Once boiling, turn the heat down to medium, adjust the lid so the pot is only partially covered, and cook until the mixture is aromatic and the cashews are very soft, about 15 minutes.
2. Transfer the sauce to a blender or food processor, and blend on high speed until you have a thin purée. Return the sauce to the pot and turn the heat to low.
3. Melt the butter in a small frying pan over medium heat. Add the ginger and garlic pastes and cook, stirring regularly, until browned, 2–3 minutes.
4. Add the browned pastes and the paprika to the saucepan with the sauce and stir to combine.
5. Once the chicken is cooked, cut it into bite-sized cubes. Add the chicken, cream, garam masala, and kasoori methi to the saucepan with the sauce. Stir to combine, cover, turn up the heat to medium-low, and let cook, stirring occasionally, to bring out the flavours, 10–15 minutes.
6. Serve immediately with rice or warm naan.

*Look for red chili powder, green chili paste, garam masala, and kasoori methi in the international section of the grocery store or at an East Indian grocery store.
**Note that tomatoes that are overly ripe will make the sauce too runny.

199

THE BIG EASY KITCHEN

In memory of
Warren Montgomery
(1979-2021)
Regina, SK

Warren Montgomery always said he was New Orleans through and through, having called the city home for years until a move to Regina in 2010. At the Big Easy Kitchen, he cooked up Southern comfort food classics like gumbo, étouffée, and jambalaya, offering an authentic taste of New Orleans, unique to YQR.

Inspired by his love of Southern home cooking, Warren started the Big Easy Kitchen in 2017 when he began making and selling gumbo and Cajun spring rolls out of his home. He later opened a restaurant in 2018, but after several months he decided to shift his focus to catering, pop-ups, and retail goods, selling ready-made meals and signature sauces at local grocery stores. In summertime he also offered crawfish boils in Regina and the surrounding area, where he would quite literally bring the party to your backyard, complete with music, a delicious crawfish feast, and a lesson on how to properly eat crawfish.

Warren was passionate about educating his customers about what authentic Cajun and Creole food tastes like, highlighting the fact that while the flavours are strong, spice is only one part of the story. His dishes featured a wide range of flavour profiles and were based on the food he grew up with, grounded in traditional recipes and cooking methods that family members had passed down for generations. In a nod to his roots, the business was named after New Orleans' nickname, the Big Easy, given to signify the city's laid-back, easygoing lifestyle.

In April of 2021, Warren passed away after contracting COVID-19. He will be remembered and missed dearly by family and friends, as well as the Regina and provincial culinary communities.

The Big Easy Kitchen's Shrimp Creole

—

» MAKES 4–6 SERVINGS
» TIME: 1 HOUR

1 cup unsalted butter
1 medium yellow onion, diced small
1 medium green bell pepper, diced small
3 stalks celery, diced small
⅓ cup all-purpose flour
1 (10 oz/284 mL) can diced tomatoes
1 (28 oz/796 mL) can crushed tomatoes
2 cups unsalted (or low-sodium) chicken stock or broth
3 garlic cloves, minced
1 Tbsp granulated sugar
1 Tbsp Cajun seasoning*
½ tsp sea salt
¼ tsp cayenne pepper
12 oz (about 25) peeled and deveined raw shrimp, fresh or if frozen, thawed**
Cooked white rice, for serving
Chopped green onion, for garnish (optional)

Shrimp Creole is a classic Louisiana Creole dish that has a warming and complex flavour. Warren always said that Cajun food should showcase the flavours of the dish upfront, followed by a slight spice kick on the back end, and this recipe does exactly that. The Creole sauce can be used as a base and works well with shrimp, chicken, or meatless options. When the Big Easy Kitchen was a restaurant, Warren typically served this as a side with catfish. At home, try it over rice, along with a cold beer or cider to balance out the bold, savoury taste.

1. Place the butter in a medium pot and melt it over low heat. Turn the heat to medium-high and add the onion, bell pepper, and celery. Cook the veggies until translucent, 10–15 minutes.
2. Add the flour and stir it into the vegetables to create a roux. Cook, stirring regularly to combine, until it begins to darken slightly, about 5 minutes.
3. Add the diced tomatoes and their juice and stir to combine with the roux. Continue to cook the mixture on medium-high heat, stirring constantly, until the roux and diced tomatoes are well blended and fully combined, about 5 minutes. Then add the crushed tomatoes, stock, garlic, sugar, seasoning, salt, and cayenne pepper. Stir to combine, turn the heat to high, and bring the mixture to a boil. Once boiling, cover the pot and turn down the heat to low. Let the Creole simmer on low heat for 30 minutes, stirring occasionally so that it does not stick to the bottom of the pot. This will give it time to thicken and let the flavours develop.
4. Stir in the shrimp, turn up the heat to medium, and cover the pot. Cook until the shrimp turn pink and are tender and cooked through, 5–10 minutes.
5. Serve immediately over rice with a sprinkle of chopped green onion (if using).

*You can buy Cajun seasoning at the grocery store, or try making your own at home. A quick Internet search will result in many homemade Cajun spice mix recipes, which typically include common household spices like garlic powder, paprika, cayenne pepper, and oregano.
**You can omit the shrimp altogether for a meatless version of this recipe, or substitute the shrimp with chicken. Use 2 boneless chicken thighs or breasts, cut into bite-sized pieces. Cook the chicken in step 4 until it is cooked through and reaches an internal temperature of 165°F (74°C), 15–20 minutes.

3422 Hill Avenue
Regina, SK S4S 0W9
(306) 584-0888
+ multiple SK locations
houstonpizza.ca

HOUSTON PIZZA

As the birthplace of what is known today as Regina-style pizza, Houston Pizza has established itself as a bit of a pizza empire in Saskatchewan. Characterized by a crust that is crispy on the outside and soft and bread-like on the inside, Regina-style pizza is loaded with all manner of toppings, stacked in thick layers and cooked to cheesy perfection.

When the Kolitsas brothers opened Houston Pizza in 1970, they weren't planning on inventing a legendary pizza—they just wanted to make a living. Originally from Greece, the four brothers—John, George, Gus, and Tony—immigrated to Canada in the early 1960s and began working at restaurants before opening their own. The first Houston Pizza location was at 3422 Hill Avenue—and is still in operation today—and had humble beginnings with a mostly take-out menu of pizza, burgers, and spaghetti.

John's son, Jim Kolitsas, says the restaurant saw barely any customers in its early months, but toward the end of the year, the city suddenly seemed to discover what it was missing. They went from zero to 100 in a matter of months, and, with orders flying in, the business took on a life of its own. They were making dough constantly and had to clear out a back storage area to accommodate seating.

They soon realized their pizza had struck a chord with the community, so when a staff member mentioned he'd like to open another location, the brothers agreed. The Moose Jaw location opened in 1979, followed by Regina's second location in 1980, and so the Houston Pizza franchise was born.

Today Houston Pizza has five Regina locations, plus restaurants in Moose Jaw, Swift Current, and Fort Qu'Appelle. Several family members still own and operate locations today, and plans for future restaurants are underway. The menu has expanded over time too, with favourites like souvlaki, dry ribs, and house-made Caesar and Greek dressings, which are popular both on salads and as dipping sauces.

The main event remains the pizza, however. In fact, it has become something of a cult classic, in part because of the focus on quality ingredients. The sauce is a handmade recipe, the dough is made from scratch,

The Kolitsas brothers stand with one of their legendary pizzas in July of 1988.
Left to right: John, George, Tony, and Gus Kolitsas.

and the pizza meats feature specific spice blends, including Saskatchewan mustard in the salami. The flavours meld together in a way unlike any other—and I'm not just saying that. Director of operations Spero Milios spends a significant portion of time packing and shipping pizzas to customers outside of Saskatchewan, who are willing to pay exorbitant shipping costs for a taste of home. Houston Pizza has come up with a method of packaging the pizzas half-cooked, along with cooking instructions, so that they can be successfully sent anywhere. Common destinations include Ontario, British Columbia, Texas, California, and Florida, but pizzas have been sent as far as Australia.

It's safe to say Regina-style pizza has a loyal following, and memorable customers over the years have included the Rolling Stones and the Barenaked Ladies. Houston Pizza has also been featured on the Food Network and CBC's *The Great Canadian Food Show*, and there have been spinoff restaurants too, some of which were opened by family or staff who got their start working at Houston Pizza.

When I asked why they called it Houston Pizza, Jim says they could never get a straight answer to this question from the founders, but the story goes that the brothers picked "Houston" off a map because it was recognizable and easy to pronounce. Such a simple beginning has fostered considerable success, and with a history of 50 years and counting, it's clear that Regina-style pizza and the Kolitsas brothers' legacy is here to stay.

Houston Pizza's All Dressed Pizza

—

Dough

1⅓ cups water, at room temperature (about 22–24°C/72–75°F)*

1 Tbsp granulated sugar

2¼ tsp instant dry yeast

3½ cups all-purpose flour

2 Tbsp canola oil

¾ tsp sea salt

Toppings

½–1 cup marinara (tomato) sauce, any kind

2½ cups shredded mozzarella cheese, divided

4½ oz sliced pepperoni

4½ oz sliced garlic sausage

4½ oz sliced salami

4½ oz sliced black forest ham

1 large green bell pepper, thinly sliced

1 small yellow onion, thinly sliced

1 cup thinly sliced mushrooms

½ cup sliced or cubed pineapple**

Houston Pizza has over 25 different pizzas. This recipe is for an at-home version of their all dressed, which is their most popular pizza. It features deli meats, vegetables, pineapple, and mozzarella, but you can change up the toppings to suit your liking and simply use this recipe as a base. Be careful not to stack the pizza *too* high (yes, even Houston Pizza admits there's a limit) so that it cooks properly. Due to the generous number of toppings, it's a ritual at Houston Pizza to cut the finished pie into squares, making it easier to eat.

DOUGH

1. Place the water, sugar, and yeast in a large bowl and whisk together until the yeast has completely dissolved.
2. Add the flour, oil, and salt to the bowl. Stir together and then, using clean hands, mix until the dough develops a smooth texture and all the ingredients are well combined.
3. Turn the dough out onto a clean, lightly floured surface and knead it into a ball for 2–3 minutes. The dough should be smooth and not sticky. Add a little bit more flour, 1 tsp at a time, if needed to reach the desired consistency.
4. Place the dough back in the bowl and cover with plastic wrap. Let the dough rise at room temperature until it has doubled in size, 15–20 minutes.

TOPPINGS AND ASSEMBLY

1. Preheat the oven to 400°F (200°C) and, if available, use the convection setting. Lightly grease a 12- to 13-inch round pizza pan with cooking spray or line it with parchment paper.
2. Once the dough is done rising, transfer it to the pizza pan and, using clean hands, slowly press it into the pan. Start with the middle, pushing it down and out evenly with the palm of your hand, until it fills the entire pan. Form a 1-inch-wide and 1-inch-thick crust around the entire perimeter, but otherwise ensure the dough is an even thickness throughout so that it cooks properly. The flat part of the dough should be about ½-inch thick.
3. Spread your desired amount of sauce on the dough, leaving the crust bare. Sprinkle about ½ cup of the mozzarella on top of the sauce. It will act as the glue to hold all the toppings in place.
4. Add the toppings to the pizza in layers, starting with the meat, followed by the vegetables, pineapple, and then the remaining 2 cups of cheese. Be sure to leave the crust bare.

5. Cook the pizza on the centre rack of the oven for 20–30 minutes. The cooking time will vary depending on the type of oven and thickness of your toppings, but the pizza is done when the crust and cheese are both golden brown. You can leave the pizza in the oven for an extra 5 minutes or so to get an even crisper crust, if desired.

6. Once the pizza is done, remove it from the oven and use a large knife or spatula to gently lift or slide it out of the pan. Place it on a cutting board, cut it into generous squares, and serve immediately.

*Check the water with an instant-read thermometer to ensure it reaches the correct temperature, which is necessary to activate the yeast.
**If using canned pineapple, drain off any excess liquid first.

SIAM AUTHENTIC THAI RESTAURANT

1946 Hamilton Street
Regina, SK S4P 2C4
(306) 352-8424
siamrestaurant.ca

As the province's only certified Thai SELECT restaurant serving authentic Thai food, Siam is unique in Saskatchewan. But when Thutchai and Siritorn Srisodsai opened Siam they had no plans for becoming certified—they just really missed Thai food. Originally from Bangkok, they initially came to Regina so that Siritorn could study at the University of Regina. When they couldn't find authentic Thai food in the city, Thutchai started cooking it himself for them to enjoy at home.

Soon the couple decided they wanted to open a restaurant, so Thutchai went to Bangkok for a few years for culinary training. He then came back to Regina and opened Siam in 2007. He created Siam's menu based on the traditional Thai dishes they grew up with and loved, and it turned out that Regina loved them too. Siam quickly became a mainstay, especially for the downtown lunch crowd, with favourites like green curry chicken,

pineapple fried rice, and, of course, the ever-popular pad Thai.

In 2018, an unassuming customer approached them after finishing his meal to ask if they had considered applying for Thai SELECT status. The customer turned out to be the Thai minister of commerce, and he actively encouraged them to start the process of certification. Becoming certified is no small feat, as the recognition comes from the Royal Thai Government after a restaurant proves that they offer a minimum of 60 percent authentic Thai food on their menu and use similar cooking methods and ingredients to those found in Thailand.

Siam received Thai SELECT status in November 2018, and the certificate hangs proudly in the restaurant's front window. Regulars who have travelled to Thailand in the past have even come back to tell Thutchai that his food is just like what they ate there—a fact he's always happy to hear.

Siam's Pineapple Fried Rice

—

» MAKES 2–3 SERVINGS
» TIME: 1 HOUR
» GLUTEN-FREE (OPTION)

1 whole large pineapple

1 cup vegetable oil, divided

2 oz sliced Chinese sausage*

2 large eggs

2¼ cups cooked and chilled jasmine rice (about 1 cup uncooked)

2 Tbsp granulated sugar, divided

2 tsp Thai seasoning sauce, divided** (gluten-free if preferred)

2 tsp soy sauce, divided (gluten-free if preferred)

1½ tsp curry powder

¾ tsp ground turmeric

7 oz boneless chicken breast (about 1 large chicken breast)

3 garlic cloves, minced

½ cup chopped (1-inch-long matchsticks) green onion

½ cup sliced yellow onion

¼ cup whole unsalted cashews

1½ tsp oyster sauce (gluten-free if preferred)

A pinch of ground black pepper

This recipe is beautifully presented in a plump, juicy pineapple filled to the brim with warm fried rice and chicken, flavoured with cashews, onion, and garlic. Thutchai has adapted the recipe by serving the chicken on top of the rice, instead of mixed together, to create two separate tastes that play off each other. The pineapple gives the fried rice a bit of a sweet and sour flavour, and, for contrast, Thutchai recommends pairing it with something spicy, like a tom yum shrimp soup or a dash of your favourite hot sauce.

1. Take the whole pineapple and slice ¼ of it off the side. Cut it to just before the stem to ensure the whole stem is left intact on ¾ of the pineapple, which will be used for the bowl. Using a small knife or a spoon, carve out the inside of the pineapple to create a bowl, and keep the other ¼ of the pineapple for later use as a lid. Cut the pineapple fruit into small chunks, about 1 × 1½ inches. You will need 1 cup chopped pineapple total. Set the chopped pineapple and the pineapple bowl and lid aside.

2. Heat 1 Tbsp of the oil in a large wok over medium heat. Add the sausage and cook on both sides until heated through, about 2 minutes per side. Set aside.

3. Add 3 Tbsp of oil to the wok, still over medium heat. Add both eggs and stir for 15 seconds. Then add the rice, chopped pineapple, and sausage, and stir together to combine.

4. Add 1 Tbsp of the sugar, 1 tsp of the seasoning sauce, 1 tsp of the soy sauce, the curry powder, and turmeric. Turn up the heat to high and stir-fry all the ingredients until heated through, about 1 minute.

5. Put the fried rice into the carved pineapple bowl, pop the lid on top, and set it aside on a rimmed baking sheet.

6. Preheat the oven to 450°F (232°C).

7. Cut the chicken into bite-sized pieces. Heat ½ cup of the oil in the wok (no need to wipe it out first) over medium-high heat, and fry the chicken until cooked through, about 5 minutes. The chicken should be golden and have an internal temperature of 165°F (74°C).

8. Move the chicken to one side of the wok and add 2 Tbsp of the remaining oil and the garlic. Turn down the heat to medium and cook for about 15 seconds. Add the green onion, yellow onion, and cashews, and mix together with the chicken and garlic. If it looks a bit dry, add the remaining 1 Tbsp of oil, but it's unlikely you'll need it. Cook until heated, about 2 minutes. If needed, you can add a little bit of cold water, about 1 tsp at a time, to prevent the ingredients from sticking to the bottom of the wok.

9. Add the remaining 1 Tbsp sugar, 1 tsp seasoning sauce, and 1 tsp soy sauce, the oyster sauce, and a pinch of ground black pepper to the wok. Turn up the heat to high and stir-fry until all the ingredients are mixed together and heated through, 3–5 minutes.
10. Put the chicken mixture on top of the fried rice in the pineapple bowl. Replace the pineapple lid. Bake the stuffed pineapple in the oven until heated through, 3–5 minutes. You can bake it a bit longer for more of a smokey flavour, but be careful that it does not burn.
11. Remove the stuffed pineapple from the oven and serve immediately.

*Look for Chinese sausage at an Asian grocery store, or substitute 2 oz of cooked deli ham, cut into small squares, for the Chinese sausage.
**Look for seasoning sauce in the international section of a grocery store or at an Asian grocery store.

Tip: The cooking portion of the method moves quite quickly, so it is best to do all chopping and measuring of ingredients prior to starting the recipe.

216

1925 Victoria Avenue
Regina, SK S4P 0R3
(306) 525-8777
cravekwb.com

CRAVE KITCHEN + WINE BAR

Crave Kitchen + Wine Bar has been a mainstay in Regina's food scene since 2006. It is known for an elevated menu that features carefully crafted and beautifully presented plates like lamb shank, duck confit, and crème brûlée. With a focus on strong, rich flavours, Crave makes a point of sourcing ingredients from provincial suppliers, including Saskatchewan Snow Beef in Caronport and Fenek Farms, outside of Regina, bringing quality to the forefront of their restaurant and catering menus.

Executive chef and managing partner Jonathan Thauberger is originally from Regina and joined the Crave team in 2012. After graduating from the Dubrulle French Culinary School in Vancouver, he spent several years working in Vancouver and the Okanagan before moving back home. He has an abundance of fine dining experience and won Gold Medal Plates Regina in 2013 and 2015, and represented YQR at the Canadian Culinary Championships in 2014 and 2016. Well seasoned, he's also the president of the Culinary Federation's Regina branch and a member of Culinary Team Canada, which competed at the 2020 IKA Culinary Olympics in Germany.

Crave is located inside a historic building which was home to the Assiniboia Club, a gentlemen's club, from 1912 until 2007. The building has tons of character, both inside and out, and in addition to the restaurant, it houses several event rooms where Crave caters weddings, private dinners, and business meetings. Their lovely patio is a popular spot, looking right onto bustling Victoria Avenue, and art from Slate Fine Art Gallery in Regina graces the restaurant's walls, showing off local contemporary artists. Crave is the perfect place to enjoy a long lunch or indulge in a slow, relaxed dinner, with its winning combination of quality ingredients, culinary distinction, and historic charm.

Crave's Mustard Potato Salad

—

» MAKES 4–5 SIDE SERVINGS
» TIME: 40 MINUTES
» GLUTEN-FREE + VEGAN
   (OPTION)

2½ lb fingerling or baby
   Yukon Gold potatoes
½ cup smooth Dijon-style
   mustard
2 Tbsp honey or agave syrup
   (use agave syrup for a
   vegan option)
2 Tbsp rice vinegar
½ cup cold-pressed canola
   oil*
2 Tbsp whole grain mustard
2 Tbsp finely diced shallot
2 Tbsp freshly chopped
   parsley (any type is fine)
Sea salt
Pickled onions, microgreens,
   and thinly sliced fresh
   radish (optional, for
   garnish)

Mustard is a staple crop in Saskatchewan, and this recipe showcases the seed in two ways: whole grain and Dijon-style. Crave's mustard potato salad has had various incarnations on both their restaurant and catering menus over the years. This version can be served warm or chilled, and it features a tangy mustard dressing that could also be used as a dip alongside a ham or a roast. The recipe is simple to make and is sure to be a crowd-pleaser at a barbeque or potluck, offering a local twist on the tried-and-true picnic classic.

1. Cut the potatoes into bite-sized pieces and place them in a medium saucepan with enough water to cover them completely. Bring to a boil over high heat, and then reduce the heat to medium and cook the potatoes until tender and cooked through, 15–20 minutes.

2. Meanwhile, prepare the dressing by whisking the Dijon-style mustard, honey, and vinegar together in a medium bowl. Slowly add the oil to the bowl, whisking the entire time, until all the oil is fully incorporated.

3. Add the whole grain mustard, shallot, and parsley, and fold them into the dressing until well combined.

4. Once the potatoes are done, drain and set them aside to cool slightly. Then transfer them to a large bowl and sprinkle with salt, to taste.

5. Pour the dressing overtop of the potatoes and mix gently to combine. Garnish with pickled onions, microgreens, or thinly sliced radish (if using). Serve immediately as a warm salad, or refrigerate, uncovered, until the salad is thoroughly chilled, to serve cold.

*A different vegetable oil, like olive oil or grapeseed oil, can be substituted for the canola oil. If you are using extra-virgin olive oil, use half olive oil, half canola oil for best results.

Crave's Duck Confit

—

Duck confit is a staple on Crave's dinner menu and a dish that executive chef Jonathan Thauberger has been serving for over 20 years. Originating in France, duck confit involves slow-cooking and storing the duck in its own seasoned, rendered fat, and then retherming (reheating in the oven) to properly crisp the skin, which results in flavourful, tender meat. It's a recipe that's meant to be savoured, and it pairs well with side dishes that have a slightly acidic taste to contrast with the duck's rich flavour. Try a side of greens with citrus or cranberry dressing or Crave's Mustard Potato Salad (page 219). Note that the duck has to cure overnight.

» MAKES 2-4 SERVINGS
» TIME: 3½-4 HOURS + OVERNIGHT TO CURE
» GLUTEN-FREE

4 duck legs, fresh or, if frozen, thawed
3 garlic cloves, minced
3 whole green cardamom pods
2 bay leaves, crushed
2 whole star anise
1 sprig of fresh basil
1 sprig of fresh rosemary
1 large shallot, sliced
1 cinnamon stick, broken into pieces
1½ Tbsp coarse sea salt*
4 cups rendered duck fat**

1. Trim the duck legs of any excess fat, and then place the legs and trimmed fat in a large bowl. Add all the other ingredients to the bowl, except for the rendered duck fat. Toss the ingredients together, ensuring all the duck legs are evenly coated with the seasoning. (Note that the basil and rosemary sprigs remain whole.) Transfer the seasoned duck legs and the trimmed fat to an airtight container and allow them to cure overnight in the refrigerator.

2. The next day, preheat the oven to 325°F (165°C).

3. If you are using rendered duck fat and it has hardened in the fridge, melt it in a medium saucepan over medium heat.

4. Place the duck legs and trimmed fat in a casserole dish that is large enough to hold everything without crowding. (All of the duck seasoning goes into the dish as well.) Pour the rendered duck fat overtop of the duck legs, cover the dish with a lid or aluminum foil, and bake until the duck legs are fork-tender but not quite falling off the bone, 2 to 2 ½ hours. Check them after 2 hours, and, if needed, put them back into the oven for the last ½ hour. By this point the meat will have also surpassed the recommended internal temperature of 165°F (75°C).

5. Remove the duck legs from the oven and allow them to cool and settle in the dish on the counter, uncovered, still in the liquid. This will take about 1 hour.

6. When the duck is cool enough to touch, preheat the oven to 425°F (220°C) and line a rimmed baking sheet with parchment paper.

7. Using tongs, remove the duck legs from the liquid and place them skin down on the baking sheet. Remove and discard any large pieces of the seasoning stuck to either side of the skin (including pieces of the bay leaves, star anise, and cinnamon stick, which are not recommend for consuming whole).

8. Cook the duck legs for 5–7 minutes, and then flip them over and cook them skin up, for another 5–7 minutes. The second cooking of the duck in this step is important to properly crisp the skin.
9. Remove the duck legs from the oven and serve immediately.

*The coarse sea salt can be substituted with 1 Tbsp fine sea salt.
**The rendered duck fat can be substituted with lard, tallow, canola oil, or olive oil.

Tip: The leftover liquid and fat from the cooking process have a very rich flavour and can be saved for future use. Strain the mixture through a fine-mesh sieve into a medium bowl and allow it to settle and cool completely at room temperature. Separate the fat from the liquid and then store them in separate airtight containers in the fridge for up to 2 weeks. The liquid can be used as the base for a soup or a sauce, and the fat can be used for cooking or for a future batch of confit.

Sourcing tip: For where to find duck legs and rendered duck fat, see the Sourcing Local Guide (page 284).

South

—

Many establishments province-wide work with ingredients grown and produced in Saskatchewan, putting concepts like farm-to-table and seed-to-table into regular practice. For several of the recipes in this chapter, the chefs and business owners make a point of sourcing ingredients directly from their communities, be it berries from a nearby grower or meat raised and butchered locally. Their efforts highlight where our food comes from and how it is grown, and allows people to sample Prairie flavours and support local food systems simply by dining out.

Although my family has a history of farming, I was raised in the city and have no direct farming experience. That said, one thing that has always been important to our family is gardening, which is perhaps one of the most direct and accessible seed-to-table connections. My grandparents' summertime pride and joy is their garden, which takes up much of the backyard and supplies us with fresh produce all season long. Likewise, my parents always plant a garden next to their raspberry patch come May, with peas, lettuce, and carrots in neat and tidy rows.

My earliest memory of the garden involves my sister, Aunya, who could always be trusted to tag along in whatever mischief I dreamed up. As kids, we often spent summers together in the backyard, turning our wooden playcentre into a house. Being the elder sister, I typically took on the motherly role in the game of house, and thus when it was time for "dinner," I would wander over to the garden to prepare what can only be described as a miserable "vegetable soup."

Grabbing an old yogurt container, I'd head straight for the carrots and yank a small fistful of the green tops, pulling a few carrots from the earth and breaking off the tops. The carrots would get a brief wash with the hose prior to being added to the soup. Next were the peas, which have long been a garden favourite of mine. Fresh peas, and maybe even the odd pod, went into the mix, followed by a few shreds of garden lettuce and a sprinkle of herbs, usually dill, for flavour, of course. The last stop before heading back to the playcentre was the garden hose, to top off the soup with a simple broth of ice-cold hose water.

Aunya was always dismayed by the soup, but would sample it begrudgingly. The one consolation was the handful of raspberries I would often pick for her for dessert. As an adult, I have a much different appreciation for how food is grown and produced, not to mention a much better understanding of why my parents were never pleased with the holes I left in the garden. Since then, I've also learned how to make a proper vegetable soup, and these days hose water never makes the cut.

Growing fresh produce in your own backyard and then using it for pickling, preserving, or your next dinner is a simple yet empowering practice. It takes patience, care, time, and energy to tend to food, whether it's grown in a garden or on a farm, and, similarly, it takes effort to establish

the relationships needed to source ingredients directly from local suppliers. Establishments in rural settings—including those in the south of
the province—are often mere kilometres away from the growers, farmers,
and ranchers they source from, helping to build a network of reciprocity
within their communities. Working with regional ingredients is an inten-
tional choice that chefs and business owners make, knowing that it not
only supports the local food system, but also ensures that quality ingredients grace your plate.

HARVEST EATERY & THE BLIND BOAR

492 Centre Street
Shaunavon, SK S0N 2M0
(306) 297-3315
eatharvest.ca

When I think of Harvest Eatery, the words "creative" and "cutting-edge" come to mind. The restaurant has been a culinary staple in Saskatchewan for years, with a menu that is innovative yet grounded in traditional comfort food. Husband and wife duo, chef Garrett "Rusty" and Kristy Thienes, are passionate about offering a memorable dining experience and continually push themselves to be at the forefront of the province's food scene.

But how exactly does a restaurant in a town of 1,800 become an award-winning culinary destination? When they opened in 2013, Kristy, who is from White Rock, British Columbia, was skeptical, but Rusty assured her if they offered food worth driving for, well, people would drive. And did they ever. Nowadays, Harvest Eatery welcomes guests from all across Saskatchewan and beyond, and the restaurant has also been a past recipient and finalist of various tourism awards.

Harvest Eatery's interior is timeless and classic, with rich, dark tones. The décor features Saskatchewan art and incorporates many second-hand and upcycled pieces. The tables are made of reclaimed threshing flooring, while the bar in their private dining room, the Blind Boar, is a receptionist desk from the dental office that previously occupied the building. The restaurant also serves as a gathering spot for the community, hosting live music, supper clubs, and a summer block party.

Rusty pours his heart and soul into every menu item and has won many awards, including Gold Medal Plates Regina in 2016. A key part of his food philosophy involves working with farmers in the Shaunavon area to support provincial food systems. His food is meant to encourage you to slow down, enjoy lively conversation, and share a meal with others, much like a harvest dinner. By reimagining classic Prairie dishes using locally sourced ingredients, Rusty says he's always working toward one overarching goal: mastering what Saskatchewan tastes like on a plate.

Harvest Eatery's Smoked Southwestern Brisket

—

» MAKES 6–8 SERVINGS +
2 CUPS MAPLE BOURBON
DEMI

» TIME: 7–10 HOURS +
30 MINUTES–1 HOUR
TO REST

» GLUTEN-FREE

Southwest Rub

½ cup smoked Hungarian
  paprika

¼ cup kosher salt

2½ Tbsp garlic powder

2½ Tbsp coarse ground
  black pepper

2 Tbsp chipotle paste, or
  1 Tbsp chipotle chili
  pepper

1½ Tbsp onion powder

1½ Tbsp ground white
  pepper

1 Tbsp cayenne pepper

1 Tbsp dried thyme

1 Tbsp dried oregano

1 Tbsp brown sugar

Brisket

1 (5 lb) beef brisket

Hickory or apple smoker
  pucks or wood (if you are
  smoking the brisket)

Maple Bourbon Demi

1 Tbsp unsalted butter

1 shallot, finely diced

1 garlic clove, minced

2 oz bourbon

¼ cup maple syrup

4 cups beef or veal stock*

This brisket has been a signature dish on Harvest Eatery's menu since the restaurant's inception. The meat is tender, succulent, and juicy, while the southwest rub has an aromatic peppery flavour that is balanced by the warm sweetness of the maple bourbon demi. It's a hearty main course that deserves to take centre stage at a barbeque, paired with sides like Mustard Potato Salad (page 219), biscuits, or creamed corn. If you have leftover brisket, try shredding it for sandwiches the next day. Rusty notes that this recipe is meant to be made slowly, so make it on a day when you can take your time and relish the process.

SOUTHWEST RUB

1. Combine all the rub ingredients in a medium bowl and mix together thoroughly with your hands, breaking up any clumps until all the spices are well combined.

BRISKET

1. Preheat a smoker to 200°F (95°C) or the oven to 250°F (120°C).
2. Lightly trim any excess sharp and protruding edges from the brisket. It should be level and smooth throughout, so that smoke and/or heat can travel evenly through all parts of the meat. Any sharp or protruding edges will burn or dry out during cooking and will need to be trimmed off later anyway.
3. Generously coat the entire brisket with the rub, using your hands to press and massage it into the meat. Use as much as you can (ideally, use all of it), because brisket is generally 50 percent fat, meaning that as it cooks, a large portion of the seasoning is rendered away with the fat. If you have any leftover rub, you can store it in an airtight container in the fridge for up to 1 week.
4. To cook the brisket in the smoker and oven: Place the brisket in the smoker with the smoker pucks or wood. Smoke it for between 1 hour and 15 minutes to 1 hour and 40 minutes, depending on the smoker. Brisket should be smoked on average for 15–20 minutes per pound. During the last 10 minutes of smoking time, preheat your oven to 250°F (120°C). Once the brisket is done smoking, remove it from the smoker and place it on a rimmed baking sheet lined with parchment paper. Transfer the brisket to the oven and cook, uncovered, on the centre rack until the internal temperature reads 200°F (95°C), 4–6 hours.

5. To cook the brisket entirely in the oven: Line a rimmed baking sheet with parchment paper and place the brisket on it. Cook the brisket, uncovered, on the centre rack of the oven at 250°F until the internal temperature reads 200°F (95°C), 6–8 hours. The total cooking time will depend on your oven, but cooking it for longer will render away more of the fat (if preferred).
6. Meanwhile, prepare the demi (below).
7. Remove the brisket from the oven and allow it to rest for 30 minutes and up to 1 hour. You can leave it uncovered or loosely cover it with aluminum foil.
8. Cut the meat into generous slices, cutting against the grain. Given that brisket is a large cut, you may have to change directions when slicing to continue cutting against the grain, depending on the size of your slices.
9. Serve immediately with the warmed demi on the side or drizzled overtop.

MAPLE BOURBON DEMI

1. Melt the butter in a large saucepan over medium-low heat. Add the shallot and cook until translucent and slightly caramelized, about 5 minutes.
2. Add the garlic and continue to cook until the shallot and garlic are browned and fragrant, 1–2 more minutes.
3. Remove the pan from the heat and add the bourbon to deglaze it. If you are using an open flame, be very careful, as it can ignite. Scrape all the brown bits from the bottom of the pan to incorporate them into the demi. (The brown bits have a ton of flavour.) Over medium heat, reduce the mixture until it is au sec (nearly dry), and then turn the heat to low and stir in the maple syrup.
4. Add the stock, bring the mixture to the brink of a boil, then turn down the heat to medium-low and simmer, stirring occasionally, for 1–2 hours. The cooking time will vary depending on your saucepan and stove, but the demi is done when it is reduced by half and coats the back of a spoon.
5. The demi is best served warm overtop of the sliced brisket. Leftover demi can be kept in an airtight container in the fridge for up to 1 week or in the freezer for up to 3 months.

*Ensure you use a real beef or veal stock. Many farmers' markets or butchers sell frozen ready-made stock, or you could make your own. Store-bought beef broth will not work the same as stock, as it lacks the marrow needed to properly thicken the demi.

Tip: Use the internal temperature of the brisket rather than the recipe's timings as your guide to doneness. The time variation in this recipe accounts for oven differences and the differences in brisket itself, which can vary greatly from one cut of meat to another. One thing to keep in mind is that you may experience a "stall," where the internal temperature seems to barely move for a time. If this happens, do not turn up the oven, but just let it continue to cook until it overcomes the stall and reaches the internal temperature of 200°F (95°C). If it takes longer to cook than the listed time, that's okay.

Sourcing tip: For where to find brisket, see the Sourcing Local Guide (page 279).

Harvest Eatery's
Whole Lotta Rosie Cocktail

—

Haskap, rhubarb, and rosehips come together in this cocktail to create a strong floral and fruit flavour with the perfect balance of sweet and tart. The vibrant, raspberry pink colour is topped with the silky foam from the shaken egg white, which provides a smooth, velvety finish. This cocktail looks and tastes like it should be nursed during a cocktail hour, while you browse an art gallery, or with vintage jazz playing softly in the background—or all of the above! It's classy, fragrant, and a bit romantic, showcasing Saskatchewan flavours with every sip.

» MAKES 1 COCKTAIL + 1 CUP SYRUP
» TIME: 10 MINUTES + 10 MINUTES TO STEEP

Rose Syrup

1 cup rosehips*
1 cup caster (superfine) sugar
1 cup water

Whole Lotta Rosie Cocktail

1½ oz Black Fox Farm & Distillery Haskap Gin**
2 Tbsp rose syrup (above)
1 Tbsp freshly squeezed lemon juice
1 Tbsp egg white (about ½ egg white)
2–3 ice cubes
A splash of soda water
3 dashes rhubarb bitters***

ROSE SYRUP

1. Place the rosehips, sugar, and water in a medium saucepan over high heat and bring to a boil. Let the mixture boil, uncovered, until all the sugar is dissolved, stirring occasionally.
2. Remove the pot from the heat and let the syrup steep on the counter, uncovered, for 10 minutes.
3. Strain the syrup through a fine-mesh sieve into a container or jar. Discard the rosehips.
4. Leftover rose syrup can be stored in an airtight container in the fridge for up to 2 weeks.

WHOLE LOTTA ROSIE COCKTAIL

1. Place the gin, syrup, lemon juice, and egg white in a cocktail shaker and shake hard until the egg white foams, about 20 seconds.
2. Add the ice cubes and shake again for about 15 seconds.
3. Strain the cocktail through a cocktail strainer or small sieve into a coupe glass or a champagne flute.
4. Add a splash of soda water and the rhubarb bitters to the glass. Serve immediately.

*Look for rosehips at an Asian grocery store or a bulk foods store.
**Black Fox Farm & Distillery is located near Saskatoon. Their Haskap Gin uses their traditional gin, Gin #3, which is then infused with tea leaves, gentian root, and juice from haskap berries grown on the Black Fox farm. Note that using a different gin in this cocktail will not yield the same results.
***Harvest Eatery recommends the rhubarb bitters from the Silk Road Spice Merchant in Calgary and Edmonton. Alternatively, look for rhubarb bitters in specialty spice shops or liquor stores.

Sourcing tip: For where to find Black Fox Farm & Distillery products, see the Sourcing Local Guide (page 282).

202 Main Street
Ogema, SK S0C 1Y0
(306) 459-7747
soloitalia.ca

SOLO ITALIA FINE PASTA INC.

Solo Italia is impossible to miss, housed in a sunny yellow Quonset with a cherry red roof on Ogema's Main Street. It's an iconic landmark that people drive from across the province to visit, all for a taste of authentic Neapolitan eats.

Husband and wife duo Marco de Michele and Tracey Johnson met while vacationing in Costa Rica in 2007, and then settled in Marco's native Italy for a few years. In 2012 they moved to Ogema, where Tracey grew up. While looking for a job, Marco decided to try making and selling pasta locally. What started as a home operation quickly grew to the point where they needed a permanent location, as the orders started flooding in. The town offered them the Quonset, which had been sitting empty for years, and after extensive renovations they opened in 2013, complete with a fresh coat of yellow paint on the building's exterior to represent pasta, and red, for tomatoes.

One day, their pasta machine broke down. While they were waiting for a replacement part to arrive from Italy, they started selling Neapolitan pizza. The pizza was met with such enthusiasm that Marco built an 8,000-pound wood oven so that they could cook pizza and other bread items the traditional way. Thanks to the wood oven, Solo Italia always smells of heavenly wood-fired pizza dough and aromatic tomato and basil.

Nowadays, their pizzas and pastas can be found across the province in grocery stores, and in warmer months, customers can enjoy fresh thin-crust pizza at picnic tables on the Quonset's front lawn. Their menu offerings are all true to their roots, based on Italian recipes that have been passed down for generations. Being authentic is something Marco and Tracey pride themselves on, and means they certainly live up to their name, Solo Italia ("Only Italy"), in every sense.

Solo Italia's Handmade Pasta

—

3½ cups durum semolina
   flour*
2 large eggs
¾ cup warm water
All-purpose flour

This recipe has been adapted from Solo Italia's pasta recipe so that it can be made either by hand or with a household pasta maker. Simple and traditional, it's made with fresh, accessible ingredients like eggs and durum semolina flour. The pasta can be cut into various widths to make fettuccine, spaghetti, or pappardelle, and can be used as a base for your favourite sauce, like ragù, marinara, or pesto. Be sure to wrap the pasta in nests after it's been cut, which prevents cracking and is an easy way to portion it out.

1. Place the semolina flour in a large bowl.
2. Place the eggs in a small bowl and whisk them lightly. Whisk in the warm water. For best results, weigh the water and eggs using grams. They should equal 250 g, which is 8⅘ oz.
3. Make a well in the flour and gradually add the water and egg mixture in small increments, mixing after each addition with a sturdy spoon or clean hands. Once almost all the liquid has been added (about 80–90 percent), mix it thoroughly for 2 minutes. If the dough appears too dry, add the remaining liquid and mix again for another 2 minutes. The dough should be relatively stiff, not dry and crumbly or so wet that it sticks to your hands. The water and flour composition can vary, so you may have to adjust the liquid measurement to attain the desired consistency.
4. Divide the dough into halves or quarters. On a clean, lightly floured surface, knead each dough ball until smooth, 3–5 minutes. Once you are finished kneading the dough balls, cover them with plastic wrap or a plastic food storage bag to prevent them from drying out when not in use.
5. Once all the dough is kneaded, place 1 dough ball on a clean, lightly floured surface. Using a rolling pin, roll out the dough, dusting it generously with all-purpose flour as you go. Allow the dough to roll over your rolling pin several times, which makes it easier to obtain a thinner pasta. The ideal dough thickness once it's rolled out is 0.5 to 1 mm. (If you have a manual pasta roller, roll out the dough, using a rolling pin, until it is 2 to 4 mm thick, and then cut it into 4-inch-wide strips. Feed the dough into the pasta roller, starting with the thickest setting and gradually working to a thinner setting until the desired thickness is reached.)
6. Using your hands, roll the thin, floured pasta dough into a long tube-shape. Using a knife, cut along the pasta roll to slice up the pasta. The width of your cut will depend on what kind of pasta you want to make. Make your slices very close together for narrower pasta shapes, like fettuccine, or cut wider pieces for something like pappardelle. Dust the pieces in flour, shake off the excess, and

then form them into nests by gently unfolding the pieces of pasta and wrapping them around your hand. Set the completed nests aside, uncovered. (Alternatively, if you have a pasta cutter, cut the pasta using the instructions for your brand of pasta cutter. Once cut, wrap the pasta in nests and proceed with cooking or freezing.)

7. Repeat with the remaining dough.

8. The pasta can be cooked immediately or frozen. To cook immediately, bring a large pot of salted water to a rolling boil on high heat and then place 6–8 pasta nests in the pot. The cooking time will vary depending on the thickness of the pasta, but it should be done after 2–5 minutes. Note that fresh pasta cooks much faster than dry packaged pasta, so watch it carefully to ensure it does not overcook. Drain the cooked pasta, add it to your favourite sauce, and serve immediately.

9. If freezing the pasta, store it in a well-sealed freezer-safe bag in the freezer for up to 3 months. When ready to use, cook the pasta from frozen. The cooking time should be about the same as for fresh.

*Solo Italia measures their flour by weight in grams for fresh pasta. If you want to make a truly authentic version of this recipe, the flour should weigh 600 g, which is a tiny bit more than 21 oz.

Sourcing tip: For where to find durum semolina flour, see the Sourcing Local Guide (page 284).

The Gallery Café
76 Fairford Street West
Moose Jaw, SK S6H 1V1
(306) 693-7600
yvettemoore.com

YVETTE MOORE GALLERY

The Yvette Moore Gallery is a gem in southern Saskatchewan, renowned for its strong commitment to the province's arts community. The gallery is the exclusive exhibition site of acclaimed artist Yvette Moore's art and is home to a collection of handcrafted works by Western Canadian artisans. If that weren't enough, there's also the ever-popular Gallery Café, their in-house restaurant.

Born in Radville, Yvette moved to Moose Jaw in 1986 to pursue a diploma in Architectural Engineering Technology. What started as a hobby eventually turned into a full-time career, as she began painting scenes depicting life on the Prairies. Her paintings showcase snapshots of both Prairie landscapes and everyday life in beautiful, vivid detail, and she's won many awards over the years, including the Saskatchewan Order of Merit in 2015 and a Senate 150th Anniversary Medal in 2017. Yvette has also illustrated three books, including the widely celebrated *A Prairie Alphabet*, for which she received the Mr. Christie's Book Award for Illustration in 1992.

In 1998, Yvette acquired the historic Land Titles Building in Moose Jaw with the intention of using it as a permanent base for her art. Built in 1910, the building is a Municipal Heritage Property and was home to the Land Titles Office until 1998. Over the years, some of the original heritage elements had been changed or renovated, so, fuelled by a passion for architecture and historical preservation, Yvette decided to restore the building. With much work to be done, family and friends were called in to help. The restoration included everything from repairing plaster on the walls to removing the suspended ceiling to reveal the original, expansive 18-foot ceiling. Many other striking details were discovered in the process, including copper-faced windows and doors, which were uncovered after helpers carefully removed layers of paint. The Yvette Moore Gallery officially opened its doors in March of 1999, just 87 days after the restoration began.

The Gallery's in-house restaurant, the Gallery Café, was introduced in May of 1999 and soon became a favourite spot in Moose Jaw for lunch and dessert. The menu focuses on wholesome Prairie dishes, including fresh salads, homemade

This photograph was taken by photographer Lewis Rice, who came to Moose Jaw in 1910 and stayed until his death in 1913. The Land Titles Building was constructed in 1910, and this photo was taken shortly after, sometime between 1910 and 1913. Today, the original building still looks very much the same as pictured here but includes an expansion to the east, added in 1922 as the rapid growth of Moose Jaw necessitated a larger office registry.

soups, and classic desserts like grandma's bread pudding and Saskatoon berry pie. In addition to the pie, their menu features an extensive list of Saskatoon berry items, including iced tea, scones, crepes, and even a Saskatoon berry sangria. Antique township maps from 1882 decorate the café's walls and the original desks from the Land Titles Office have been repurposed into tables. Many of the café's recipes have been lovingly created and refined over time by Yvette and her children, who are very much involved in the running of the gallery. Yvette's daughter Sarah Moore is the creative director and manages communications and creative design, as well as the Gallery Café. Tyler Moore, Yvette's son, runs their in-house framing business.

Since 1999, the Yvette Moore Gallery has grown to be a central hub for arts, history, and tourism, drawing visitors year-round who marvel at the gallery and building alike. The building itself is simply magnificent, matched only by the award-winning artwork inside. It's certainly the perfect place to spend a day, offering visitors the chance to step back in time and get lost in a world where history and art collide.

The Gallery Café's
Saskatoon Berry Pie

—

» MAKES 1 (9-INCH) PIE
» TIME: 2 HOURS 30 MINUTES

Saskatoon berry pie is the quintessential Prairie pie, and it's a mainstay on the Gallery Café's dessert menu. Sarah sources Saskatoons from Prairie Berries (see page 291) in Keeler for this recipe, which has been adapted over time by café staff and generations of women in the Moore family. Yvette even has a painting titled *Saskatoon Pie – Just Like Mom's*, which depicts her daughters preparing a pie at the kitchen table. With a jammy berry filling and a flaky, golden brown crust, Saskatoon berry pie is best served topped with a generous scoop of vanilla ice cream, alongside coffee or tea.

Crust

1½ cups all-purpose flour
1 tsp granulated sugar
¼ tsp sea salt
¼ tsp baking powder
½ cup shortening
1 egg, divided
1 tsp white vinegar
Ice-cold water

Saskatoon Berry Filling

4 cups fresh or frozen
    Saskatoon berries*
¼ cup granulated sugar
3 Tbsp cornstarch
1 tsp instant or minute
    tapioca
⅓ cup berry-flavoured juice
    (mixed berry or grape
    juice works well)
4 tsp unsalted butter or
    margarine, divided into
    ½ tsp portions
1 Tbsp lemon juice

For serving

Vanilla ice cream or
    whipped cream (optional)
Icing sugar (optional)

CRUST

1. Preheat the oven to 350°F (180°C).
2. Place the flour, sugar, salt, and baking powder in a large bowl. Stir together to combine.
3. Using a pastry cutter, cut the shortening into the flour mixture until it forms crumbs, about the size of peas.
4. Place the egg in a small bowl, whisk it lightly, and divide it into two portions.
5. Place one half of the whisked egg and the vinegar in a liquid measuring cup, and whisk them together until well combined. Then add ice-cold water to the measuring cup, so that the total volume of the half egg, vinegar, and water equals ⅓ cup of liquid. The total amount of water will vary slightly depending on the size of your half egg.
6. Make a well in the flour and pour the liquid mixture into it. Use a pastry cutter to mix it all together gently, just until a solid dough is formed. Be careful not to overmix.
7. Form the dough into a ball and place it on a clean, lightly floured surface. Separate the dough into two portions and set half aside for the top crust. Use a rolling pin to roll out the other half of the dough to about 10 inches in diameter.
8. Fit the crust loosely into a 9-inch pie pan by gently pressing it down. There's no need to grease the pan. Set it aside while you prepare the filling.

SASKATOON BERRY FILLING

1. Place the berries, sugar, cornstarch, and tapioca in a medium bowl, and stir together to combine. Pour the mixture into the pie crust and spread it around evenly.
2. Pour over the berry juice. Dot the butter portions evenly overtop of the berries, then sprinkle evenly with the lemon juice.

TO ASSEMBLE

1. Use your fingers to wet the edges of the bottom crust by dabbing a little bit of water on your hands and then pressing it into the dough.

2. On a clean, lightly floured surface, roll out the top crust using a rolling pin until it is about 10 inches in diameter. Fold the crust in fourths (in half and then over again to form a triangle) and then cut a small tip from the point of the triangle. Make narrow ¼-inch-long slits along the straight edges of the folded crust, so that the pie can vent while baking. Gently lay the crust over the berries (with the tip in the centre) and unfold it into place. Seal the wet edges of the top and bottom crusts by pressing them together, firmly but gently, with your fingers. You can either flute the edges, fold them over, or leave them as a straight edge and trim the excess.

3. Take the remaining half of the whisked egg and, using a pastry brush, lightly brush it on top of the entire pie.

4. Place the completed pie on a rimmed baking sheet (this ensures there are no leaks and makes it easier to remove from the oven) and bake on the centre rack of the oven until the crust is golden brown, 1 hour.

5. Remove the pie from the oven and let it cool and set at room temperature for at least 1 hour prior to cutting. Serve the pie with vanilla ice cream or whipped cream and a sprinkle of icing sugar on top (if using).

*If you're using frozen berries, don't thaw them before using them in this recipe.

Tip: The pie can be baked immediately or frozen once assembled. To freeze it, prepare the pie in an aluminum pie pan as above, but don't apply the egg wash. Transfer to a large freezer-safe bag and freeze for up to 3 months. When you're ready to bake, brush egg wash over the frozen pie and bake directly from frozen, per the method. You might need to add a few more minutes to the baking time.

Sourcing tip: For where to find Saskatoon berries, see the Sourcing Local Guide (page 291).

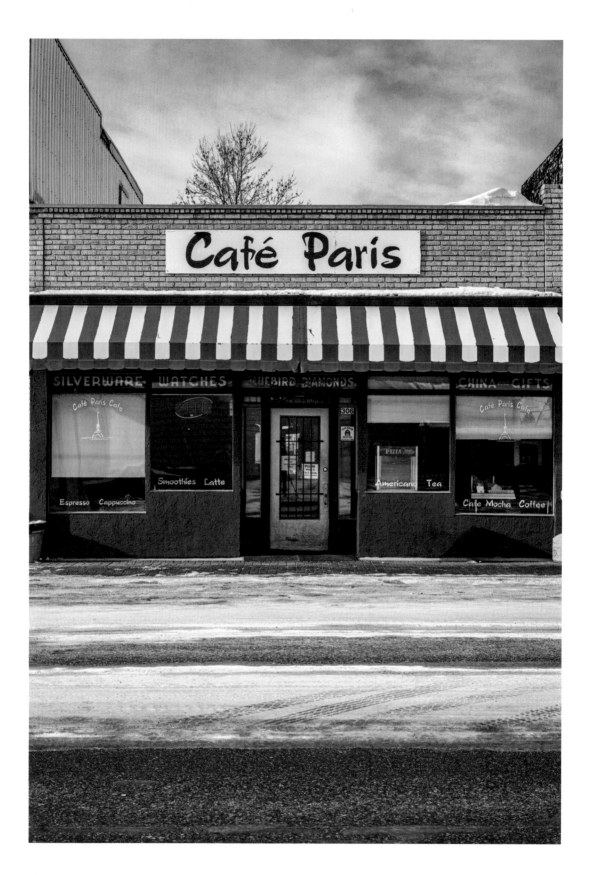

306 Main Street
Gravelbourg, SK S0H 1X0
(306) 648-2223
facebook.com/
CafeParisGravelbourg

CAFÉ DE PARIS

With strong French roots, the town of Gravelbourg is known for offering "a touch of Europe on the prairies," and Café de Paris is no exception. With a made-from-scratch menu focusing on bistro-style eats, Café de Paris is a French-inspired café, complete with a courtyard patio and charming, eclectic décor.

Owner André Chevrier was born and raised in Gravelbourg, and he opened the café in 2005, after operating several coffee shops in Vancouver. He lives and works in Vancouver, so the café has been leased by different people over the years, but it has always had a strong focus on specialty coffees, light lunches, and dreamy desserts. In the fall of 2020, André brought in chef Pat Church to expand the menu and add dinner service. Originally from Alberta, Pat has worked in restaurants all over Canada, from the Okanagan to southern Ontario, and likes to be adventurous, flipping the menu and adding new features regularly. Their extensive wine selection is the perfect complement to menu favourites like Turtle cheesecake, fresh salads, and prime rib.

Inspired by his visits to France, André modelled Café de Paris on a traditional French café, including the courtyard patio, which is distinctly European, complete with greenery, string lights, and a beautiful fountain. The inside décor features black-and-white checkered wood flooring, and antiques such as posters for French liquor advertisements from the early 1900s, and a large gold gilt mirror from a château in France. The café is attached to a gift shop, Styles for Home, which has a large selection of giftware and locally made goods, and is popular with visitors who come to dine and shop. All in all, Café de Paris is a quaint and cozy spot, bringing a little bit of *je ne sais quoi* right to Saskatchewan's south.

Café

PARIS

Sesame salmon 24

filed I charred stir-fry I basmati rice I pest

Café de Paris' Pickled Golden Beet and Goat Cheese Salad

—

» MAKES 4–6 SERVINGS +
3 CUPS PECANS + 1¼ CUPS
DRESSING

» TIME: 2 HOURS + 1 HOUR
TO CHILL

» GLUTEN-FREE

Pickled Golden Beets

6 medium-sized golden
(yellow) beets, washed
and peeled

1 cup water

½ cup apple cider vinegar

½ cup white vinegar

¼ cup maple syrup

**Orange Creamsicle
Candied Pecans**

2 large egg whites

1 tsp water

1 tsp orange extract

½ tsp vanilla extract

½ tsp Kahlúa

1 cup granulated sugar

1 tsp ground cinnamon

1 tsp grated tangerine or
orange zest

3 cups shelled whole
unsalted pecans

Honey Lime Dressing

1 cup mayonnaise

Juice of 2 limes

3 Tbsp honey

1 tsp red wine vinegar

Salad

6 pickled golden beets

10 cups mixed greens or
2 heads of lettuce,
washed and dried

This salad is a popular item on the Café de Paris' menu from chef Pat Church. The pickled golden beets and orange Creamsicle candied pecans are the stars of this salad, and they contrast with the goat cheese and honey lime dressing perfectly. It's a beautifully presented dish that works well for a lunch date or as a dinner party starter. Golden beets have a more muted, slightly sweeter taste than red beets, but you can substitute with red beets, if desired. Leftover pecans can be used as toppers for other salads or eaten on their own as a snack—they're delicious.

PICKLED GOLDEN BEETS

1. Place all the ingredients in a medium saucepan, stir gently to combine, and bring to a boil over high heat. Once boiling, turn down the heat to medium and cook the beets, covered, until tender and cooked through, about 25 minutes.

2. Remove the pan from the heat and let cool, uncovered, at room temperature.

3. Transfer the beets and the liquid to an airtight container and refrigerate for at least 1 hour. You can also make the beets ahead of time and let them chill in the fridge for 2–3 days prior to serving.

ORANGE CREAMSICLE CANDIED PECANS

1. Preheat the oven to 300°F (150°C). Line a rimmed baking sheet with parchment paper.

2. Using a stand mixer fitted with the whisk attachment or an electric mixer, whisk the egg whites and water together on high speed until they start to foam, about 1 minute. Add the orange extract, vanilla extract, and Kahlúa, and whisk again until stiff peaks form, 3–5 minutes.

3. In a small bowl, mix together the sugar, cinnamon, and zest, and then, using a spatula, gently fold them into the egg white mixture until well combined.

4. Add the pecans to the bowl and stir to combine with the coating, ensuring all the pecans are evenly covered.

5. Spread the coated pecans evenly on the prepared baking sheet and bake on the centre rack of the oven until crispy and golden brown, 30–40 minutes. Flip them over every 8–10 minutes to ensure they cook evenly and do not burn.

1 medium cucumber, diced
small or sliced into
ribbons
1 cup orange Creamsicle
candied pecans (above)
½ cup sweetened dried
cranberries
Honey lime dressing (above)
2 medium carrots, julienned
½ cup crumbled goat cheese

6. Remove the pecans from the oven and let them cool completely at room temperature before using.

HONEY LIME DRESSING

1. Whisk together the mayonnaise and lime juice in a small mixing bowl. Add the honey while continuing to whisk. Once combined, whisk in the vinegar until fully incorporated.

SALAD

1. Remove the pickled golden beets from the fridge and drain the liquid. Slice each beet into thin pieces, about ¼-inch thick. You can also leave some beets whole, if preferred.
2. Place the mixed greens, cucumber, pecans, and dried cranberries in a large mixing bowl. Add the honey lime dressing, to taste, and then toss the salad to combine.
3. Portion the salad into individual serving plates, or keep it in the large bowl to serve as a whole. Top with the beets, carrots, and goat cheese. Serve immediately.

Tip: The orange Creamsicle candied pecans can be substituted with store-bought candied pecans, if preferred.

Sourcing tip: For where to find golden (yellow) beets, see the Sourcing Local Guide (page 286).

240 James Street North
Lumsden, SK S0G 3C0
(639) 392-7132
freebirdeats.com

FREE BIRD

JP Vives grew up in Lumsden and is passionate about contributing to the community, noting that Free Bird is truly a neighbourhood place. Situated on Lumsden's main street, the restaurant is surrounded by businesses it sources from, including the local bakery and butcher shop.

Before opening Free Bird in 2019, JP studied professional cooking at Camosun College in Victoria, British Columbia, and worked at the former Bodega Tapas Bar in Regina and Congress Beer House in Saskatoon. As Free Bird's co-owner and head chef, he works alongside his mom, Pam, tag teaming the daily operations. The focus is on doing "common food uncommonly well," and JP likes to put his own twist on well-loved eats like eggs Benedict, fried chicken, and sourdough pizza.

Free Bird is located in a building that previously housed a hardware store and a grocery store, which JP remembers visiting when he was growing up. He opted to keep some of the familiar elements like ceiling track lighting, which used to be a light display, and a mock deck near the front, which is now used as a stage for live music. The décor is industrial, a nod to the building's previous incarnations, with lots of dark tones and textures like leather booths, suede chairs, and wood tables and floors. One wall is lined with antique doors from the early 1900s, which were found in Pam's garage and repainted, while a signature painting of rapper the Notorious B.I.G. by JP's sister adds a splash of brilliant colour to the front entrance.

Lumsden itself is worth visiting, as it is one of the province's most charming boutique towns, surrounded by the rolling hills of the stunning Qu'Appelle Valley. JP says his ultimate goal with Free Bird is to support the community and put Lumsden on the map by offering soul-satisfying comfort food.

Free Bird's Shakshuka

—

Shakshuka is a dish with Middle Eastern and North African origins, and it is one of Free Bird's most popular brunch items. It's an ideal brunch comfort food, perfect for sharing family-style or for enjoying the day after a night out. This recipe features eggs cooked to your liking overtop of a spicy sauce of tomatoes, bell peppers, onion, and juicy, seared chorizo, finished with fresh green onions and parsley. It's exactly the type of dish you want to cozy up with on a cold winter day, and it pairs well with ale or dark beer, plus thick slices of your favourite bread for scooping.

» MAKES 4-6 SERVINGS
» TIME: 1 HOUR
» GLUTEN-FREE

2 Tbsp olive oil
1 lb precooked chorizo sausage, sliced into rounds*
2 medium bell peppers (any colour), diced medium
1 medium yellow onion, diced medium
3 garlic cloves, minced
3 Tbsp chili powder
2 Tbsp ground cumin
2 Tbsp paprika**
2 (each 28 oz/796 mL) cans of crushed or diced tomatoes
Sea salt
Ground black pepper
4-6 large eggs***
1 baguette or sourdough loaf, for serving (gluten-free if preferred)
⅓ bunch of fresh parsley (any type), chopped
3-4 green onions, sliced on a bias

1. Preheat the oven to 400°F (200°C).
2. Place the oil in a 12-inch cast-iron pan or frying pan over medium heat.
3. Add the chorizo and cook, stirring regularly, until all the slices are evenly seared, 5-7 minutes.
4. Add the bell peppers and onion, and sauté with the sausage until the peppers and onion are tender and soft but not caramelized, 5-8 minutes.
5. Turn down the heat to medium-low and stir in the garlic. Add the chili powder, cumin, and paprika, and stir to combine.
6. Stir in the tomatoes and their juice. Turn the heat up to medium-high to bring the mixture to a hard simmer, but don't let it boil. Once it's simmering hard, turn down the heat to medium-low and add salt and pepper to taste. Let the mixture simmer on medium-low heat for 5 minutes.
7. If you're using a cast iron pan, crack the eggs on top of the tomato mixture and then, using oven mitts, put the pan into the oven. If you're using a frying pan, spray a casserole dish with cooking spray and transfer the tomato mixture to the casserole dish. Crack the eggs on top of the mixture and place the casserole dish in the oven. Cook for 15-25 minutes, depending on how you prefer your eggs. For runny eggs, cook for 15 minutes, and for firm eggs, cook for 25 minutes or more, if needed. Check the dish occasionally to ensure the eggs do not overcook. If you are using a casserole dish, you may need to cover it loosely with aluminum foil to ensure the eggs cook evenly.
8. Meanwhile, slice and toast the bread. Line a rimmed baking sheet with parchment paper and lay the slices of bread on it. Drizzle them with some oil and then toast them in the oven for 8-10 minutes. Flip the slices over at the halfway point to ensure they toast evenly.
9. Once the shakshuka and bread are done, remove them from the oven and sprinkle the parsley and green onions overtop of the shakshuka. Serve immediately family-style.

*Chorizo can be substituted with precooked andouille or Italian sausage.
**You can use your favourite paprika for this recipe, but note that hot paprika will make the dish very spicy.
***Allow 1 egg per person.

THE ROLLING PIN BAKERY & CAFÉ

316 Souris Avenue
Weyburn, SK S4H 0C7
(306) 842-1220
facebook.com/
TheGermanSK

The Rolling Pin is a charming bakery and café in the southeastern corner of the province, specializing in German breads, pastries, and lunch fare. The business was originally opened by Annika Enslin, who is a fourth-generation baker and grew up learning the trade from her parents and grandparents at their family bakery in Germany.

Annika and her husband, Andre, moved to Saskatchewan in 2012. Initially, Annika began baking just because she really missed the homemade bread she grew up with, but she soon began to sell her bread at Weyburn's Open Air Market. She quickly realized there was a real interest in freshly baked bread and other goodies, and in 2019, she opened The Rolling Pin's permanent location.

After running the bakery and café for a couple of years, in 2021, Annika sold the business to Anie Alpuerto, who is from the Philippines and had already been working at The Rolling Pin. Anie had always dreamed of owning a bakery and has years of baking experience, especially in cake decorating. She has plans to add some Filipino offerings to the menu, to go alongside Annika's well-loved recipes.

The interior of The Rolling Pin is light and pretty, with soft pinks, white, and natural wood tones. The wall behind the front counter features open shelves where the daily breads are on display, just as they would be in a traditional German bakery. The breads themselves are a real treat, dusted with flour and baked to golden-brown perfection. Hearty, homemade soups are always on the lunch menu, served alongside pretzel buns, and the front display is always well-stocked with beautiful cakes and pastries, all decorated in a dainty and delicate fashion. Whether you stop by for lunch or to pick up a sweet treat, one thing's for sure: you're getting the best of the best, with recipes that have been tried and tested for generations.

The Rolling Pin's Borscht

—

» MAKES 8-10 SERVINGS
» TIME: 1 HOUR 45 MINUTES
» GLUTEN-FREE + VEGAN
(OPTION)

¼ cup unsalted butter or
margarine (use margarine
for a vegan option)
2 medium yellow onions,
diced small
2 medium red bell peppers,
diced small
2 large carrots, grated
2 medium beets, peeled and
grated
¼ cup tomato paste
8 cups water
6 medium yellow potatoes,
diced medium
3 cups shredded green
cabbage
2 garlic cloves, minced
2 tsp paprika (any type)
½ tsp sea salt
½ tsp ground black pepper
¼ cup chopped fresh dill,
plus more for garnish
Sour cream, for serving
(omit for a vegan option)

Borscht is a customer favourite at the Rolling Pin, with many regulars stopping by specifically on days when it's the feature soup. This recipe is from Olga Telizki, who is from Russia and works at the Rolling Pin, and it's a staple that's been in her family for years. Simple yet satisfying, borscht is loaded with vegetables like carrots and beets, which give it a rich burgundy colour. Top your borscht with a generous dollop of sour cream and a sprinkle of chopped dill, along with a side of fresh bread for dunking in the flavourful, piping hot broth.

1. Place the butter in a large pot and melt it over medium heat. Add the onions, bell peppers, carrots, and beets, and cook, stirring regularly, until soft, about 10 minutes.
2. Stir in the tomato paste. Cook, stirring constantly so that is does not burn, until the tomato paste is well combined, 2-3 minutes.
3. Add the water, potatoes, cabbage, garlic, paprika, salt, and pepper. Stir to combine and turn the heat up to medium-high to bring the borscht to a boil. Once boiling, turn down the heat to medium-low, partially cover the pot, and let the borscht cook, stirring occasionally, until all the vegetables and potatoes are soft and cooked through, 30-40 minutes.
4. Turn down the heat to low and stir in the dill. Add more salt and black pepper to taste, if needed.
5. Serve the borscht immediately with a sprinkle of fresh dill and a dollop of sour cream overtop (if using).
6. Leftover borscht can be frozen in an airtight container for up to 3 months. To reheat, add the borscht and a little bit of water to a pot over medium heat, stirring occasionally, until it is completely thawed and cooked through.

Tip: The method moves quite quickly, so it is best to finish all chopping and grating prior to starting the recipe.

NIGHTJAR DINER CO.

325 Central Avenue North
Swift Current, SK S9H 0L5
(306) 773-2749
nightjardiner.co

Nightjar Diner is the perfect intersection of old meets new, reinventing the tried-and-true Prairie diner with modern touches and creative eats. Co-owners Derek Sandercock and Shaun Hanna wanted to contribute to the province's food scene by crafting an elevated dining experience, but in a familiar setting.

Originally from Swift Current, Shaun moved back in 2011 after some time in academia. He was looking for a creative outlet when a mutual friend, Sarah Galvin, introduced him to Derek, who was working for Black Bridge Brewery and shared a passion for food. At first, the three of them decided to host a pop-up restaurant called Farm + Table in the city's market square, offering a series of five-course dinners with a focus on local ingredients. The pop-ups received such strong support that in 2017 they won a Swift Current Business Excellence Award for best start-up or new business.

Using that momentum, Derek and Shaun opened Nightjar Diner in 2018, named after a family of birds found in Saskatchewan. Nightjars eat during twilight, which they felt was a fitting metaphor for a diner that opens close to midday. The design of the restaurant is minimalist, with diner-inspired elements, including a wraparound booth that lines the front windows and cerulean bar stools that look straight out of the 1950s. Food is served on delicate antique dishes that were donated by the community, which gives a cozy, sentimental nod to a bygone era.

Although you'll find meat and potatoes on the menu, Derek and Shaun are keen on raising the bar, whether it's adding arugula and truffle oil to a diner trope like a meatball sandwich, or sourcing Saskatchewan Speckle Park beef for their burgers. It's all very nostalgic, yet they manage to bridge comfort and innovation, simultaneously pushing boundaries and bringing you back to a treasured past.

266

Nightjar Diner's S'more

—

» MAKES 8–10 SERVINGS
» TIME: 1 HOUR + 3 HOURS TO FREEZE

White Chocolate Graham Crumb

1½ cups crushed graham cracker crumbs

⅔ cup dry skim milk powder, divided

2 Tbsp cornstarch

2 Tbsp granulated sugar

½ tsp fine sea salt

¼ cup melted unsalted butter

2 Tbsp whipping (35%) cream

4½ oz white chocolate

Grand Marnier Chocolate Semifreddo

2 cups cold whipping (35%) cream

1½ oz Grand Marnier*

½ tsp fine sea salt

4 egg yolks

½ cup + 1 Tbsp granulated sugar, divided

3 Tbsp water

5½ oz dark chocolate, 65% cocoa or higher

Topping

Marshmallow Fluff

Nightjar's S'more is an elevated take on the campfire classic, with a cold, creamy base of chocolate semifreddo—a half-frozen Italian dessert somewhere between mousse and ice cream—topped with gooey marshmallow and a crunchy, sweet white chocolate graham crumb. This dessert is an all-time customer favourite at Nightjar, and when Derek and Shaun tried taking it off the menu, they were met with everything from disappointment to a poem on a postcard lamenting its removal (they still have the postcard!). The semifreddo and graham crumb can both be prepared ahead of time or even made as a dessert in their own right.

WHITE CHOCOLATE GRAHAM CRUMB

1. Preheat the oven to 325°F (165°C). Line a rimmed baking sheet with parchment paper.
2. Mix together the graham crumbs, ⅓ cup of the dry skim milk powder, the cornstarch, sugar, and salt in a medium bowl until well combined.
3. Place the melted butter and cream in a small bowl and stir together to combine. Pour it overtop of the dry mixture and stir together, ensuring all the graham crumbs are evenly coated. The mixture should clump into small clusters and hold its shape if you squeeze it with your hands.
4. Spread the crumb mixture evenly onto the prepared baking sheet and then bake, 10–12 minutes. Mix every 3–4 minutes to brown the mixture evenly.
5. Remove the graham clusters from the oven and let them cool completely at room temperature. Break up any large clumps into chickpea-sized pieces.
6. Place the graham clusters in a medium bowl and mix them with the remaining ⅓ cup of dry skim milk powder.
7. Melt the white chocolate in a small bowl in the microwave at 20-second intervals, stirring between each interval, until completely melted.
8. Pour the melted white chocolate overtop of the graham clusters in the bowl. Toss to coat and then allow them to dry fully at room temperature.
9. Once dry, store them in the freezer in an airtight container until you're ready to use them. The white chocolate graham crumb can be made in advance and frozen for up to 1 month. They can be eaten frozen or thawed at room temperature prior to using.

GRAND MARNIER CHOCOLATE SEMIFREDDO

1. Place the cream, Grand Marnier, and salt in the bowl of a stand mixer fitted with the whisk attachment (or use a large bowl and a handheld electric mixer). Beat on medium-high speed until stiff peaks form, 5–7 minutes. Scrape down the sides of the bowl to make sure all the cream is incorporated and then cover the bowl with plastic wrap and refrigerate. If you used a stand mixer bowl, transfer the whipped cream to a different bowl or to an airtight container to refrigerate, as the stand mixer bowl is needed in the next step. Rinse and dry the bowl and the whisk attachment or electric mixer beaters prior to starting the next step.

2. Place the egg yolks and the 1 Tbsp of sugar in the bowl of a stand mixer fitted with the whisk attachment (or use a medium bowl and a handheld electric mixer). Beat the eggs and sugar on medium-high speed until light, fluffy, and pale yellow, 5–7 minutes.

3. Place the remaining ½ cup of sugar and the water in a small saucepan over medium heat. Swirl the water into the sugar using a spoon to dissolve it into a syrup. Heat the syrup, uncovered, until an instant-read thermometer shows the syrup reaching 245°F (118°C), stirring regularly so that it does not burn. Given that there is not much liquid, you may need to tilt the pot to be able to measure the temperature correctly.

4. Remove the syrup from the heat and slowly drizzle it into the egg yolk mixture. Beat on medium-low speed until the mixture is very fluffy and roughly at room temperature.

5. Melt the dark chocolate in a small bowl in the microwave at 20-second intervals, stirring between each interval, until completely melted and fluid. Immediately pour it slowly into the egg yolk mixture. (Do not let the chocolate sit at all prior to mixing or it will begin to harden and not mix well.) Use a handheld whisk to mix it together until the melted chocolate is fully incorporated.

6. Remove the Grand Marnier whipped cream from the fridge and add it to the egg yolk/chocolate mixture in three equal additions. For the first addition, whisk the two mixtures together until fully incorporated. The second and third additions can be done more gently, folding the cream in with a spatula until fully combined.

7. Portion the semifreddo into 8–10 individual serving jars (Mason jars work nicely), or freeze the entire mixture in a 9- × 5-inch loaf pan lined with plastic wrap or wax paper. Cover the jars or loaf pan with plastic wrap or lids and freeze for at least 3 hours. If you leave it in the freezer for more than 3 hours, it will have a firmer texture, more similar to ice cream or gelato.

1. Remove the semifreddo from the freezer. If you froze it in a loaf pan, gently lift the plastic wrap or wax paper from the pan to remove it, and then cut it into 8 or 10 slices.
2. Place 1 slice of semifreddo on a plate, or take an individual jar portion, and top with a heaping spoonful of the white chocolate graham crumb and a generous dollop of Marshmallow Fluff to taste. Nightjar uses a blowtorch on the marshmallow for a perfect toasted flavour, but the dessert is equally great with or without that option. Once assembled, serve immediately.
3. The semifreddo can be kept in an airtight container or covered tightly and stored in the freezer for up to 1 month. When you are ready to use it, assemble the dessert and serve immediately.

*Grand Marnier gives the semifreddo a subtle chocolate and orange flavour, but you can use other liqueurs. Nightjar suggests Kahlúa for a coffee flavour or crème de menthe for mint.

Nightjar Diner's Flat-Land-Hattan Cocktail

—

» MAKES 1 COCKTAIL + ½ CUP SEA BUCKTHORN JUICE
» TIME: 15 MINUTES
» GLUTEN-FREE (OPTION) + VEGAN (OPTION)

Sea Buckthorn Juice

1 cup fresh or thawed sea buckthorn berries

Flat-Land-Hattan Cocktail

1½ oz rye
¼ oz sweet vermouth
¼ oz dry vermouth
1 Tbsp sea buckthorn juice (above)
1 Tbsp simple syrup
4 dashes Angostura aromatic bitters
2–3 ice cubes
1–2 maraschino cherries, for garnish

The Flat-Land-Hattan is a twist on a Manhattan, using both sweet and dry vermouth and a sea buckthorn juice, which gives the drink its orange and yellow colour. Sea buckthorn berries are grown on the Prairies and are slightly sour, with subtle notes of citrus and tropical fruit. At Nightjar, this cocktail features a sea buckthorn verjus, which is the juice pressed from unripe berries. If you can source unripe berries for this recipe, you can use them for the juice, but ripe ones will still work due to sea buckthorn's naturally tart flavour. This cocktail pairs well with seafood, sharp cheeses, cured meats, or—Shaun adds jokingly—Netflix.

SEA BUCKTHORN JUICE

1. Place the sea buckthorn berries in a food mill or a blender and crush them on low speed until they are well blended and form a fine pulp.
2. Transfer the pulp to a fine-mesh sieve set over a bowl or jar and strain, pressing down with the back of a spoon to extract maximum juice.

FLAT-LAND-HATTAN COCKTAIL

1. Place all the cocktail ingredients, except for the cherries, in a cocktail shaker. Shake hard for 15–20 seconds, and then strain into a martini or coupe glass.
2. Garnish with the cherries and serve immediately.

Tip: If you want to make this recipe gluten-free and/or vegan, ensure the brands of alcohol you use for the rye, sweet vermouth, and dry vermouth are gluten-free and/or vegan friendly.

Sourcing tip: For where to find sea buckthorn berries, see the Sourcing Local Guide (page 291).

2 Fraser Avenue
Craven, SK S0G 0W0
(306) 731-2223
facebook.com/
641grillandmotel

641 GRILL & MOTEL

641 Grill & Motel really is the perfect place to eat, drink, and stay, as it offers classic comfort food in an inviting, eclectic setting, with a motel right next door. The business takes its name from Craven's history, when the 641 grid road used to run right in front of the restaurant, before Highway 20 was built.

Kali and Matthew Eddy opened 641 in 2015, with the goal of revitalizing the town's restaurant and motel. The Eddy family operates a ranch in the Craven area and brought a strong focus on local ingredients to the table, including sourcing beef from their ranch. In 2021, they sold the business to Bikramjit (Bill) and Parminder (Pam) Singh, who have over 30 years of experience in the hospitality industry. Originally from India, the couple have owned and operated many restaurants in Saskatchewan, including in Vibank, Montmartre, and downtown Regina. Pam is 641's chef and has always had a passion for cooking, while Bill runs the business side and enjoys bartending when he can.

When you walk into 641, there's an immediate feeling of comfort—and not just because of the food. The restaurant is decorated with warm, natural tones and rustic elements, including antique tractor seats and a collection of licence plates dating back to the 1920s. Menu favourites include their burgers, homemade flatbread, and butter chicken, which Pam added after she and Bill took over. The beef still comes from the Eddy family ranch whenever possible, and many other ingredients are sourced from suppliers in the area too, including Last Mountain Distillery and Jerky Boys Meats in Lumsden. Many customers make the trip from Regina and the surrounding area just for a bite to eat, especially in summertime when the patio is open. It's the ideal spot to enjoy delicious food, alongside your favourite drink, looking right onto the surrounding Qu'Appelle Valley.

641 Grill & Motel's
Craven Burger

—

» MAKES 6-8 BEEF PATTIES +
  1½ CUPS SAUCE
» TIME: 30 MINUTES
» GLUTEN-FREE (OPTION)

Fancy Sauce

1 cup mayonnaise
½ cup ketchup

Beef Patties

1½ lb lean ground beef,
  fresh or if frozen, thawed
1 egg
1 tsp garlic powder
1 tsp sea salt
1 tsp ground white pepper
1 tsp Worcestershire sauce
Vegetable oil, for pan-frying

Recommended Toppings*

Hamburger buns, toasted
Cheese (1 slice per burger)
Lettuce
Sliced tomato
Pickles
Battered or grilled onion
  rings (2 rings per burger)
Bacon (2 slices per burger)

The Craven burger is 641's house burger, loaded with delicious toppings like crisp lettuce, bacon, and battered onion rings, all piled on top of their house-made hamburger buns. This recipe features the beef patties from the Craven burger, plus their version of fancy sauce, a mayonnaise-and-ketchup-based condiment. The Craven burger is a perfect option for summertime gatherings or a weekend at the lake, and is best served alongside fresh-cut french fries.

FANCY SAUCE

1. Place the mayonnaise and ketchup in a small bowl and stir to combine. Refrigerate until you are ready to serve the burgers.

BEEF PATTIES

1. Place the beef, egg, garlic powder, salt, pepper, and Worcestershire sauce in a large bowl. Using either clean hands or a spoon, mix together until all the ingredients are well combined.

2. Shape the beef into burger patties by hand. You want them about ½-inch thick and the diameter of a hamburger bun. Place the patties on a plate or rimmed baking sheet.

3. Heat a large frying pan over medium heat, and add enough oil to coat the bottom of the pan. Once the pan is hot, place the patties in the pan, leaving a little bit of space between them. Depending on the size of your pan, you may have to cook them in batches. Cook the burgers on one side until browned, 5–7 minutes, and then flip them over and cook them on the other side, another 5–7 minutes. The patties are done when they are evenly browned on both sides and have reached an internal temperature of 160°F (71°C). (Alternatively, you can cook the burgers on the barbeque preheated to about 375°F (190°C). Cook them on both sides, until the internal temperature is reached.)

TO ASSEMBLE

1. Once the burgers are cooked, place a slice of cheese on the top side of the burgers to melt it while they're still in the pan (if using).

2. Spread a generous layer of fancy sauce on both halves of the hamburger bun. Place the cooked burger on the bottom half, and then add your preferred toppings. Serve immediately.

*These are all the toppings on 641's Craven burger, but you can switch up the toppings to your liking. For a gluten-free option, use gluten-free hamburger buns and grilled onions.

Top Your Burger the Saskatchewan Way

Saskatchewan is home to many producers who create handcrafted toppings and condiments, perfect for adding a little bit of provincial flair to your dinner table. Grab some freshly baked hamburger buns from your local bakery, ground meat from your local butcher, and one or more of these toppings, and you've got yourself a made-in-Saskatchewan burger!

1 ▸ Saskatoon Berry Style Gourmet Mustard

WHERE IT'S FROM: Gravelbourg Gourmet Mustard / gravelbourgmustard.ca

WHERE IT'S MADE: Saskatoon.

WHERE TO FIND IT: Province-wide! Visit their website for a full list of retailers or to order online.

OTHER OPTIONS: Their gourmet mustards come in 10 flavours, including Garlic, Smokin' Barbeque, and Honey Dill.

2 ▸ Judd's Hot Sauce – Citrus Heat

WHERE IT'S FROM: Paperback Beverage Co. / paperbackbevco.ca

WHERE IT'S MADE: Southey.

WHERE TO FIND IT: Local & Fresh in Regina, Miller Market in Melfort, the Wandering Market in Moose Jaw, and their online store.

OTHER OPTIONS: Judd's Worcester-Style BBQ Sauce—it's vegan and gluten-free, too!

3 ▸ Applewood Smoked Raw Milk Cheese

WHERE IT'S FROM: Saskatoon Spruce Raw Milk Cheese / saskatoonspruce.com

WHERE IT'S MADE: Osler.

WHERE TO FIND IT: Saskatoon, Regina, Moose Jaw, Lloydminster, Osler, Petrofka, and Melfort. Visit their website for a full list of retailers or to order online.

OTHER OPTIONS: Try their Caerphilly Style cheese, the original Saskatoon Spruce Raw Milk Cheese.

4 ▸ Roasted Garlic and Dill Hummus

WHERE IT'S FROM: Hanes Hummus / haneshummus.com

WHERE IT'S MADE: Saskatoon.

WHERE TO FIND IT: Saskatoon, Regina, North Battleford, Prince Albert, Moose Jaw, and Waskesiu Lake. Visit their website for a full list of retailers or to order online.

OTHER OPTIONS: Their Moroccan Seven Spice Hummus features a blend of seven spices, or try their Hot Date Hummus—equal parts spicy and sweet.

5 ▸ Buffalo Sauce

WHERE IT'S FROM: Miss Hélène's Gourmet Foods Ltd. / misshelenes.ca

WHERE IT'S MADE: Makwa.

WHERE TO FIND IT: Province-wide! Visit their website for a full list of retailers or to order online.

OTHER OPTIONS: Miss Hélène's makes eight different sauces, including Kentucky Bourbon, Raspberry Chipotle, and Black Maple.

6 ▸ Dill Pickle Kraut

WHERE IT'S FROM: Naturally Amped Fermented Foods / naturallyamped.com

WHERE IT'S MADE: Saskatoon.

WHERE TO FIND IT: Saskatoon, Regina, North Battleford, Lloydminster, Melfort, Martensville, and Moose Jaw. Visit their website for a full list of retailers or to order pickup from the Fermentery in Saskatoon.

OTHER OPTIONS: Naturally Amped makes several varieties of kraut and kimchi, including Prairie Summer Kraut, Beet Zinger Kraut, and Bridge City Kimchi.

7 ▸ Caramelized Onion Bacon Jam

WHERE IT'S FROM: Hillside Food Inc. / hillsidefood.ca

WHERE IT'S MADE: Duval.

WHERE TO FIND IT: Saskatoon, Regina, Southey, Moose Jaw, and Strasbourg. Contact Hillside Food for a full list of retailers or order online through their website.

OTHER OPTIONS: Try their Chili Lime Mustard or Corn Bacon Salsa.

8 ▸ Old Fashioned Red Sauce (Ketchup)

WHERE IT'S FROM: Deadly Dan Sauces / deadlydan.com

WHERE IT'S MADE: Saskatoon.

WHERE TO FIND IT: Saskatoon, North Battleford, Hudson Bay, and Creighton. Visit their website for a full list of retailers or to order online.

OTHER OPTIONS: Deadly Dan also makes seven different hot sauces—try Tropic Thunder or Burning Berry.

9 ▸ Green Pepper Jelly with Golden Tequila

WHERE IT'S FROM: Triple H Homestead / triplehhomestead.net

WHERE IT'S MADE: Hudson Bay and Crooked River.

WHERE TO FIND IT: Moose Jaw, Southey, Prince Albert, Battleford, Porcupine Plain, Crooked River, and Hudson Bay. Contact Triple H Homestead for a full list of retailers or order online through their website.

OTHER OPTIONS: Triple H Homestead makes 17 different flavours of pepper jelly, plus several spice mixes perfect for burgers, including Santa Fe and BBQ Rib Rub.

10 ▸ Rhubarb Relish

WHERE IT'S FROM: Petrofka Orchard / petrofkaorchard.com

WHERE IT'S MADE: Blaine Lake.

WHERE TO FIND IT: On site at Petrofka Orchard or at SaskMade Marketplace in Saskatoon.

OTHER OPTIONS: Try their Sweet-N-Spicy Apple Mustard or Sweet-N-Smokey Apple BBQ Sauce, both made with fresh apples.

11 ▸ Vegan Kimchi

WHERE IT'S FROM: Baechu Kimchi / baechukimchi.ca

WHERE IT'S MADE: Saskatoon.

WHERE TO FIND IT: Regina, Saskatoon, Moose Jaw, and Emerald Park. Visit their website for a full list of retailers or to order online.

OTHER OPTIONS: Baechu also makes Extra Spicy Kimchi with fresh Thai chili peppers.

12 ▸ Campfire BBQ Sauce

WHERE IT'S FROM: Campfire Grill Handcrafted Foods Inc. / campfiregrill.ca

WHERE IT'S MADE: Regina.

WHERE TO FIND IT: Province-wide! Contact Campfire Grill for a full list of retailers or order online through their website.

OTHER OPTIONS: Add Campfire Grill's All Purpose Steak House Seasoning and Rub to your burger for maximum flavour.

Sourcing Local Guide

I've compiled this guide as a supplementary resource to help you track down ingredients you're unlikely to find at your local grocery store and some where a high-quality version will yield better results. I have also made notes within the recipes about where to look for less common ingredients. Between the two, you should be able to find everything you need to make these recipes.

The idea for this guide came about during the recipe-testing process, when it was brought to my attention that some ingredients were challenging to find, especially if they weren't in season. (It did not help that we were testing the recipes in the middle of winter!) With a little effort, however, all of these items can indeed be sourced in Saskatchewan. The process of gathering ingredients can even become a memorable experience—picking Saskatoon berries, foraging spruce tips, or driving to a nearby farm are all wonderful ways to see and experience the province.

This guide is not exhaustive by any means, as I have only selected a handful of sources for each ingredient. It is meant as a starting point, and I have tried to provide options that are geographically diverse, whenever possible. If you are not close to any of the listed sources—or even if you are—you can always start an ingredient search by checking with local businesses or the farmers' market in your area. Many of the recipes in this book also use other ingredients that can be sourced locally, but I did not include them in this guide because they are easy to find (wild rice, pulses, cranberries, mustard, etc.). There are countless locally owned and operated farms, small businesses, and more in Saskatchewan that offer top-quality products. I encourage you to seek them out and support them year-round, be it for a recipe in this book or otherwise.

ÁRBOL CHILI PEPPERS AND TOMATILLOS

For both the Salsa Verde and Salsa Roja recipes (pages 189 and 190) you need an árbol chili pepper, which you will likely have to source from a Mexican or Latin American grocery store. The Salsa Verde recipe also requires tomatillos, which may be available at your local grocery store, depending on the time of year.

Heliotrope Organic Farm
Lumsden / heliotropefarm.com
»Heliotrope Farm products are available seasonally at the Regina Farmers' Market, the Regina Beach Farmers' Market, and Dad's Organic Market in Regina. They also have a weekly bin service for vegetables in the summer. Their tomatillo season begins around the second week of August.

Latinos Market Saskatoon

5-3010 Diefenbaker Drive, Saskatoon, SK S7L 7K2 / (306) 979-2448

»Latinos Market sells both árbol chili peppers and tomatillos, when in season.

Regina Productos Latinos Store

1211 Park Street, Regina, SK S4N 2E7 / (306) 565-6140 / reginaproductos.com

»Regina Productos Latinos Store sells both tomatillos and árbol chili peppers. They also deliver locally in Regina and have an online store.

BEEF BRISKET

I have included beef brisket in this guide because sourcing a quality cut of meat for Harvest Eatery's Smoked Southwestern Brisket (page 233) will result in a better final product. A great place to look for brisket is your local butcher, or you may want to check if there are any cattle ranches nearby that sell meat directly.

Box H Farm

Gladmar, SK S0C 1A0 / (306) 815-7191 / boxhfarm.ca

»Box H Farm offers three pick-up locations: at their farm by appointment, in Estevan at Encompass Fitness from November to April, and in Regina at Body Fuel Organics.

Cool Springs Ranch

Endeavour, SK S0A 0W0 / (306) 547-4252 / coolsprings.ca

»Cool Springs Ranch offers two delivery routes. The Regina route goes through Regina, Fort Qu'Appelle, Yorkton, and Canora, and the Saskatoon route loops through Saskatoon, Humboldt, Watson, and Kelvington.

Pine View Farms (see profile on page 294)

Osler, SK S0K 3A0 / (306) 239-4763 / pineviewfarms.com

»Pine View Farms offers the option to purchase directly from their farm, and many retailers province-wide carry their products, including locations in Saskatoon, Regina, Moose Jaw, Melfort, Prince Albert, La Ronge, Swift Current, and Warman.

Prairie Meats

Multiple locations / prairiemeats.ca

»Prairie Meats is a Saskatchewan business with three locations in Saskatoon, two in Regina, and one in Prince Albert. See their website for a full list of location addresses and phone numbers.

Ranch House Meat Company Inc.

473 Centre Street, Shaunavon, SK S0N 2M0 / (306) 297-4050 / ranchmeats.ca

»Ranch House has a retail store, custom processing, and meat-cutting services.

BISON ROAST

Depending on the time of year, bison may be available at your local grocery store. However, for Wanuskewin's Bison Bannock Pockets (page 143), it is best to use a bison round roast, chuck roast, or rib eye roast, which you may need to source directly from a supplier.

Bison Ridge Farms (see profile on page 280)

Prince Albert, SK S6V 5R3 / (306) 930-6760 / bisonridgefarms.com

»Bison Ridge Farms delivers to Prince Albert and Saskatoon, but you can also contact them directly about the possibility of delivery outside of these two locations. Their products are also available at retail stores in Prince Albert, Saskatoon, and Melfort.

Bison Ridge Farms

Bison Ridge Farms is a family-owned and -operated farm and bison ranch, located 10 minutes outside of Prince Albert. The business is owned by Denver and Becky Johnson, alongside Becky's family, who have operated an adjacent grain farm for years.

Located along the North Saskatchewan River, the farm is home to natural grasslands and a herd of wood bison. The Johnsons are keen on using the natural landscape to its fullest potential, and one of their key priorities is the sustainability of both the herd and land. They employ practices like rotational grazing, which gives the plants time to repropagate and improves the health of the surrounding grasslands.

Bison Ridge Farms offers a variety of fresh and frozen bison products, including individual cuts like brisket, steaks, and roasts, and prepared products like sausages, burgers, and jerky. They also have a meat subscription program, or you can purchase a quarter or an eighth of a whole animal in bulk. Visiting the farm is encouraged but by appointment only, and they deliver weekly to Saskatoon and Prince Albert. You can also find a full list of where to buy their products on their website, which includes several retail locations in Saskatoon, Prince Albert, and Melfort.

Bulk Cheese Warehouse

732 Broadway Avenue, Saskatoon, SK S7N 1B4 / (306) 652-8008 / bulkcheese.ca

»I have purchased a bison roast from Bulk Cheese in the past. If you call ahead and speak to someone in the meat department, they can tell you what they have in stock.

Erickson Bison Farms Ltd.

Central Butte, SK S0H 0T0 / (306) 796-7884 / ericksonbisonfarms.ca

»Erickson Bison Farms offers pickup from their farm store in Central Butte. Contact them directly for information.

Original Family Farm

Outside Saskatoon / (306) 222-4413 / On Facebook

»Original Family Farm products are available at retail locations in Regina and Saskatoon, including at the farmers' markets in both cities.

Quill Creek Farms

303 Railway Avenue, Watson, SK S0K 4V0 / (306) 287-0303 / quillcreekfarms.ca

»Quill Creek Farms is a specialty grocery store in Watson that sells bison and other meat products. The bison is supplied by their ranch, Quill Creek Bison, which is located near Quill Lake.

BLACK FOX FARM & DISTILLERY PRODUCTS

245 Valley Road, Saskatoon, SK S7K 3J6 / (306) 955-4645 / blackfoxfarmanddistillery.com
»Black Fox Farm & Distillery products (see profile on facing page) are available on site at their distillery, through their online store, or at many liquor stores province-wide. They deliver within Saskatoon and ship to the rest of Saskatchewan. Visit their website for a list of retailers (including in other provinces).

CANNOLI SHELLS

Cannoli shells are a bit tricky to find. I contacted many specialty European grocery stores in Saskatchewan in an attempt to track them down, and, in the end, I only found two locations that carry them, one in Saskatoon and one in Regina. If you do not live in either of these cities, you may have to plan ahead and buy the shells the next time you are there or, alternatively, you can likely find them online. If you want to be really creative, you can also make them at home. A simple Internet search will yield several recipes that are a great starting point.

Beppi's Gelato

1-616 10th Street East, Saskatoon, SK S7N 1B5 / (306) 227-2214 / beppis.ca
»Beppi's is primarily a handmade gelato and sorbetto shop, but they also have a small Italian grocery selection, which includes cannoli shells.

Black Fox Farm & Distillery

Black Fox Farm & Distillery is an award-winning distillery known for innovative spirits that showcase Prairie flavours. Owners John Cote and Barb Stefanyshyn-Cote are fifth-generation farmers and operated a grain farm prior to opening Black Fox, bringing a unique agricultural perspective to distilling.

Black Fox's handcrafted spirits include gins, whiskies, and liqueurs, all made in single-original small batches. Many of their products feature quintessential Saskatchewan flavours, like their Haskap Gin, Mustard Gin, and Sour Cherry Liqueur. They also offer specialty and limited edition products, including a Boreal Mint Gin, which features wild mint and juniper berries from Saskatchewan's north, and Mingle, a gin and wine spritzer they created in collaboration with Living Sky Winery in Perdue. John and Barb are committed to sustainability through all their initiatives, including crop rotation for soil sustainability and reusing nearly 95 percent of their water.

Located just outside of Saskatoon, Black Fox is a popular spot for seasonal events, including tastings, live music, flower festivals, and an autumn pumpkin patch. Their products are all available on site at the distillery, through their online store, or you can find a list of where to purchase on their website, which includes retail locations both in and out of province.

Italian Star Deli

1611 Victoria Avenue, Regina, SK S4P 0P8 /
(306) 757-6733 / italianstardeli.com
»Italian Star Deli sells cannoli shells both in
packages and in bulk.

DIEFENBAKER TROUT

Quality, fresh Diefenbaker trout is
important for Ayden Kitchen & Bar's
Dill-Cured Diefenbaker Trout (page 149)
because the fish is cured and not cooked.
Look for Diefenbaker trout at your local
butcher or at a specialty fish and seafood
store.

Bev's Fish & Seafood Ltd.

801 15th Street East, Prince Albert, SK S6V 0C7 /
(877) 434-7477 / bevsfishandseafood.ca
»Bev's Fish & Seafood has two locations in
Prince Albert and sources fish directly from
Saskatchewan lakes.

Charlie's Seafood Market

1-1810 8th Street East, Saskatoon, SK S7H 0T6 /
(306) 955-7127 / charliesseafood.ca
»Charlie's Seafood Market is located in
Saskatoon and has a large selection of fish and
seafood.

Pacific Fresh Fish

3005 13th Avenue, Regina, SK S4T 1P1 /
(306) 525-9147 / pacificfreshfish.ca
»Pacific Fresh Fish is located in Regina and
also delivers to southern Saskatchewan. See
their website or call for delivery details.

Pine View Farms – *see Beef Brisket for*
contact information

DUCK LEGS AND RENDERED DUCK FAT

On occasion I have spotted both duck
legs and rendered duck fat at grocery
stores in Saskatoon, so you may be
able to find them at your local grocery
store. After searching for more direct
sources, however, it appears that duck
legs and rendered duck fat are not overly
common, even at butcher shops. Even
so, it would be worth checking with your
local butcher to see if they have duck legs
or fat, or can order them in.

Bulk Cheese Warehouse – *see Bison Roast*
for contact information
»Bulk Cheese in Saskatoon sells both duck legs
and rendered duck fat.

Butcher Boy Meats Ltd.

2136B Robinson Street, Regina, SK S4T 2P7 /
(306) 781-6913 / butcherboymeatsltd.com
»Butcher Boy in Regina sells both duck legs
and rendered duck fat.

Summit Meats & Sausage

3-1418 Central Avenue, Saskatoon, SK
S7N 2H2 / (306) 978-8838 / summitmeats.com
»Summit Meats & Sausage in Saskatoon sells
duck legs.

DURUM SEMOLINA FLOUR

Durum semolina flour is ideal for Solo
Italia's Handmade Pasta recipe (page 241).
Look for it at your local grocery store, or
if there is a natural, organic, or bulk foods
store in your city or town, they may carry
it. I could not find any sources that make
durum semolina flour locally, so if you
cannot find any, use durum flour, which is
available from the following sources.

Daybreak Mill (see profile on page 287)
North Portal, SK S0C 1W0 / (306) 927-2695 /
daybreakmill.com
»Daybreak Mill products can be ordered
online through their website and are available
at retailers in Saskatoon, Regina, Denzil,
Rocanville, Weyburn, Melfort, Estevan,
Coronach, Windthorst, and Carnduff.

Nunweiler's Flour Company
Hague, SK / (888) 726-2253 /
nunweilersflour.com
»Nunweiler products can be ordered online
through their website and are available
at retailers in North Battleford, Rosthern,
Nipawin, Watrous, Humboldt, Yorkton, Moose
Jaw, Weyburn, Regina, and Saskatoon.

Pure T Organics
Regina, SK / (306) 757-7012
»Pure T Organics products are available
through the Regina Farmers' Market online
store or at the seasonal outdoor market most
Saturdays.

FIDDLEHEADS

Fiddleheads are most commonly found in
Saskatchewan in the spring (mid-April to
early June). They can be tricky to source,
however, and I was unable to track down
any retailers that carry fiddleheads year-
round. It is best to check for them at your
local farmers' market in springtime. The
following sources have either had them
in the past, when in season, or may be
able to help you find some. If fiddleheads
are unavailable or not in season, use
the substitution listed in the recipe for
Calories' Wild Rice Risotto (page 165).

Brian Giesbrecht
»Brian is a local forager who sells fiddleheads
in season at the Saskatoon Farmers' Market
and to the Wandering Market in Moose Jaw.
Check with the markets for more information.

Local Market YQR
1377 Hamilton Street, Regina, SK S4R 2B6 /
(306) 209-1978 / localmarketyqr.ca
»The Local Market in Regina has had
fiddleheads at their market events in the past.
Check with them for availability.

SaskMade Marketplace
1621 8th Street East, Saskatoon, SK S7H 0T2 /
(306) 955-1832 / saskmade.ca
»SaskMade has had fiddleheads in past. They
are located in Saskatoon but also deliver to
Regina.

White Fox Gold Harvesting
White Fox, SK / (306) 276-2495 /
facebook.com/torchriver
»White Fox Gold Harvesting picks and sells
wild produce, including fiddleheads and
mushrooms, when in season. It is best to
contact them directly for availability and
information on how to buy.

GOLDEN (YELLOW) BEETS

Golden beets may be available at your
local grocery store, when in season (late
June or early July), but they are much
more difficult to source than red beets. If
you cannot find them or they are not in
season, use the substitution listed in the
recipe for Café de Paris' Pickled Golden
Beet and Goat Cheese Salad (page 253).

Daybreak Mill

Daybreak Mill is located in the southeastern corner of the province in North Portal, near Estevan. Home to a stoneground flour mill, Daybreak offers grains, flours, and cereals all grown and sourced in Canada. They are also certified organic, meaning all their products are non-GMO and are produced, processed, and packaged without any chemicals, herbicides, pesticides, fumigants, or preservatives.

Daybreak Mill was started in 1963 as Scheresky Mill, named for its owner Alvin Scheresky, who was an advocate for organic agriculture in Saskatchewan. Today the mill is owned by Nicole Huriet, who grew up on an organic farm and has a passion for natural, quality products. Daybreak offers a variety of whole grains, flours, legumes, and pantry products, including golden flax, quinoa, durum flour, pastry flour, and lentils. Many of their products showcase heritage grains like red fife, spelt, and einkorn, and they also offer a number of hearty breakfast cereals, including their popular vegan Daystart Cereal, which features four grains and sunflower seeds.

Many Saskatchewan restaurants and bakeries source ingredients from Daybreak, and their products can be found at retail locations in all of the Prairie provinces. You can view a full list of retail locations on their website or order through their online store. Saskatchewan retailers include SaskMade Marketplace in Saskatoon, New Life Organic Foods in Denzil, Nutters Everyday Naturals in Melfort, and Old Fashion Foods in Weyburn and Regina.

Heliotrope Organic Farm – *see Árbol Chili Peppers and Tomatillos for contact information*

Kangro Gardening
Yorkton, SK S0A 4P0 / (306) 620-8335 / kangro.ca
»Kangro Gardening products are available seasonally at the Yorkton Farmers' Market or from their farm store, which is located just outside Yorkton.

Northwood Farm
Hafford, SK S0J 1A0 / (306) 549-0004 / northwoodfarm.ca
»Northwood Farm products are available seasonally at the Saskatoon Farmers' Market, the Wandering Market in Moose Jaw, on site at their farm, or through their online store.

Spring Creek Garden
Outlook, SK S0L 2N0 / springcreekgarden.ca
»Spring Creek Garden products are available seasonally at the Little Market Box in Saskatoon, Robertson Valley Farm just outside of Saskatoon, the Regina Farmers' Market, and a number of other seasonal market locations in Saskatoon (see Spring Creek's website for a full list).

LAST MOUNTAIN DISTILLERY PRODUCTS

70 SK-20, Lumsden, SK S0G 3C0 /
(306) 731-3930 / lastmountaindistillery.com
»Last Mountain Distillery products are available on site at their distillery in Lumsden. They have an online store but all online orders are for pickup in Lumsden only. Several retailers province-wide carry their products and a full list of retail locations is available on their website.

MUSHROOMS (CHANTERELLE AND MOREL)

Finding fresh chanterelle and morel mushrooms can be a bit of a challenge, but it is possible when they are in season come spring and summer. If you are making Calories' Wild Rice Risotto (page 165) when chanterelles or morels are not in season, use the substitution listed in the recipe.

Boreal Heartland (see profile on page 289)
319 Husky Avenue, Air Ronge, SK S0J 3G0 /
(306) 425-4778 / borealheartland.ca
»Boreal Heartland sells both fresh and dried chanterelles and morels. Fresh chanterelle and morel mushrooms are available seasonally at the Little Market Box in Saskatoon, the Wandering Market in Moose Jaw, and Local & Fresh in Regina. A full list of retailers is available on their website, and it is best to inquire with individual retailers about what is available.

White Fox Gold Harvesting - *see Fiddleheads for contact information*

NORTHERN PIKE (JACKFISH)

If you or someone you know fishes regularly, chances are you will have access to freshly caught northern pike. For Picaro's Northern Pike Fish Tacos (page 117), you can use fresh or frozen fish (thawed first), so there's some flexibility there.

Bev's Fish & Seafood Ltd. – *see Diefenbaker Trout for contact information*

Charlie's Seafood Market – *see Diefenbaker Trout for contact information*

Boreal Heartland

Boreal Heartland is an Indigenous-owned and -operated company located in Air Ronge, named for the Canadian boreal forest. The company specializes in foraging and processing wild plants exclusive to the boreal, including golden Chanterelle mushrooms from Saskatchewan's north, which are world-renowned for their flavour and texture.

With a focus on sustainable practices, Boreal Heartland maps out where they forage in order to track their harvest. To ensure sustainability they follow a rule of thirds, in which one-third of an area is designated for harvest, one-third is left for animals and birds, and one-third is left for the plants to repropagate. Boreal Heartland is also a social enterprise and works alongside local Indigenous foragers, offering training in Good Agricultural Collection Practices (GACP) and purchasing the wild goods that foragers gather.

Boreal Heartland products include fresh and dried golden chanterelles and morels, herb packets, frozen cranberries, and loose-leaf teas, which are made with foraged herbs and plants like wild mint, rosehip, and birch leaf. Their products are available at a number of retailers province-wide, including in La Ronge, Melfort, Kamsack, Moose Jaw, Prince Albert, Regina, Saskatoon, and Swift Current. A full list of retail locations for dried goods and tea is available on their website, and you can also purchase their products through their online store.

Fonos Fish

»Fonos Fish is operated by Jon Fonos, and his products are available at the Little Market Box (see page 295) in Saskatoon. You can visit in-store or order online through the Little Market Box website. Fonos Fish offers several types of fish caught in Saskatchewan, and everything is filleted and frozen individually.

Pacific Fresh Fish – *see Diefenbaker Trout for contact information*

Pine View Farms – *see Beef Brisket for contact information*

PORK BELLY

Sourcing quality pork belly is important for the Dam Smokehouse's Jerk Pork Belly (page 27) to ensure a decent ratio of meat to fat. You can always check with your local butcher first to see if they have pork belly or are able to bring it in.

Butcher Boy Meats Ltd. – *see Duck Legs and Rendered Duck Fat for contact information*

Grovenland Farm

Lanigan, SK S0K 2M0 / (306) 365-3037 / grovenlandfarm.ca

»Grovenland is at the Lanigan Farmers' Market from July through September and delivers monthly to Regina and Saskatoon. You can also contact them directly to arrange delivery in Lanigan, Watrous, Nokomis, and Humboldt.

Pine View Farms – *see Beef Brisket for contact information*

Prairie Meats – *see Beef Brisket for contact information*

Ranch House Meat Company Inc. – *see Beef Brisket for contact information*

SASKATOON BERRIES

Saskatoon berries can be found at many locations province-wide, most commonly at orchards or farms that offer a U-Pick service. They are trickier to find in the off-season, so pick them in the summer and freeze them for later use.

Crystal Beach Orchards

Harris, SK S0L 1K0 / (306) 270-5699 / crystalbeachorchards.ca
»Crystal Beach offers Saskatoon berries, raspberries, and dwarf sour cherries, all of which are available through their U-Pick or available pre-picked at their on-site retail outlet. Visit their website or call ahead for seasonal availability.

Prairie Berries Inc.

Keeler, SK S0H 2E0 / (306) 513-8411 / prairieberries.com
»Prairie Berries offers a number of Saskatoon berry products, including frozen Saskatoon berries. Their products are available year-round through their online store or at retailers in Moose Jaw, Prince Albert, Saskatoon, Regina, Yorkton, Swift Current, Davison, and Gravelbourg.

Prairie Dome

Yorkton, SK S3N 2V6 / (306) 782-7297 / prairiedome.com
»Prairie Dome offers a U-Pick for Saskatoon berries and strawberries. Their U-Pick is by appointment only.

Rhodes' Raspberries and Black Currants

Saskatoon, SK, S7K 3J6 / (306) 934-6748 / rhodesraspberries.ca
»Rhodes' offers Saskatoon berries, sea buckthorn berries, raspberries, and black currants, all of which are available frozen or at their summertime U-Pick. Visit their website or call for seasonal availability.

SEA BUCKTHORN BERRIES

There are a few places in the province that offer sea buckthorn berries or have a sea buckthorn U-Pick. They are trickier to find in the off-season, so pick them in the summer and freeze them for later use.

Nvigorate (Northern Vigor Berries Inc.)

Kamsack, SK / (306) 955-2319 / nvigorate.ca
»Nvigorate is an organic sea buckthorn company that sells a number of sea buckthorn products, including frozen berries from their orchard. Their products are available year-round at retailers in Saskatoon, Regina, Moose Jaw, and Foam Lake.

Rhodes' Raspberries and Black Currants

– *see Saskatoon Berries for contact information*

SOUR (TART) CHERRIES

Sour cherries, also known as tart cherries or dwarf cherries, are available at a few U-Pick sites throughout the province. They are trickier to find in the off-season, so pick them in the summer and freeze them for later use.

Crystal Beach Orchards – see *Saskatoon Berries for contact information*

Everyday Farms
Clavet, SK S0K 0Y0 / (306) 290-6636 / everydayfarms.ca
»Everyday Farms offers a tart cherry U-Pick when in season, as well as frozen tart cherries year-round. To purchase frozen cherries, contact them directly.

Naturally Nice Orchard & Market
Meadow Lake, SK S9X 1Z3 / (306) 236-6858 / naturallynice.ca
»Naturally Nice grows a variety of fruits and vegetables, including sour cherries. Their produce is available seasonally at the Meadow Lake Farmers' Market, Loon Lake Farmers' Market, and directly from their orchard.

SPRUCE TIPS

I have searched high and low to find a source in-province that sells spruce tips consistently, but to no avail. The best options are to ask at your local farmers' market if there are any vendors that can source spruce tips for you or forage them yourself. In Saskatchewan, the spruce tip season begins in the spring, typically late May or early June. Spruce tips are bright green, denoting new growth, and may have a brown papery husk on their very tip, which can be removed once picked. When you are foraging them, be sure to avoid over-picking from a single tree or single area. For Mabel Hill's North SK Spruce Cocktail (page 21), you can also use a different type of edible evergreen tree tip, rather than strictly spruce, depending on what is available. Once picked, wash and dry the spruce tips and then store them in an airtight container in the fridge for up to 1 month or freeze them in a tightly sealed freezer-safe bag to extend their shelf life. When testing Mabel Hill's recipe in the off-season, I sourced frozen spruce tips out of province and ordered them online, which may also be an option available to you. If you are new to foraging spruce tips, there are many excellent resources online and in print that provide more specific information on what to look for and how to forage properly.

STUMBLETOWN DISTILLING PRODUCTS

20-1905 Quebec Avenue, Saskatoon, SK S7K 1W3 / (306) 952-0691 / stumbletown.ca
»Stumbletown Distilling products are available on site at their distillery in Saskatoon or through their online store. They ship within Saskatchewan and to a number of other provinces across Canada. Their products are also available at liquor stores across Saskatchewan.

WOLF WILLOW WINERY PRODUCTS

Rudy No. 284, SK S0L 2N0 / (306) 867-9463 / wolfwillowwinery.ca
»Wolf Willow Winery products are available on site at their winery, which is located about 20 minutes north of Outlook, or through their online store. Their wines are also available at a number of retailers in Outlook, Saskatoon, and Regina, and you can find a complete list of retailers on their website.

Pine View Farms

Throughout the process of researching and interviewing for this book, Pine View Farms came up repeatedly. Many restaurants province-wide—including several featured in these pages—source meat from Pine View and will tell you that the quality is second to none. Pine View's offerings include beef, pork, lamb, chicken, fish, and turkey, and they also have a monthly meat subscription program featuring a variety of products.

Located 20 minutes outside of Saskatoon near Osler, Pine View Farms is owned by Kevin and Melanie Boldt and family, the fourth generation to operate the farm. In 1901, Kevin's great-grandfather bought the farmyard and started what is now Pine View Farms. The focus at Pine View is on observing holistic and sustainable practices in accordance with their All Natural Protocol, which ensures that all animals are raised humanely, fed a vegetarian diet, and given year-round access to the outdoors, and that no hormones or antibiotics are used. Everything is processed on site and much of the processing is done by hand, following a nose-to-tail philosophy that reduces waste by ensuring the whole animal is used.

Many retailers across the province carry Pine View's products, including locations in Saskatoon, Regina, Moose Jaw, Melfort, Prince Albert, La Ronge, Swift Current, and Warman. A full list of where to buy is available on Pine View's website. You can also order directly from them or purchase from them on site at the farm.

GENERAL RESOURCES

The following sources are mentioned in this guide as retailers that stock one or more of the listed ingredients. They are also great general resources to check with if you are looking for a specific item or want to shop local to support Saskatchewan producers and growers.

The Little Market Box

808 16th Street West, Saskatoon, SK S7M 5Y4 / (306) 361-8400 / thelittlemarketbox.com
»The Little Market Box in Saskatoon offers both in-store shopping and an online store for locally made and produced goods, including meat, produce, dry goods, coffee, and chocolate. They also deliver within Saskatoon.

Local Market YQR / Local & Fresh

1377 Hamilton Street, Regina, SK S4R 2B6 / (306) 209-1978 / localandfresh.ca
»Local Market YQR offers market events and a market delivery service called Local & Fresh to Regina and the surrounding area. They work with numerous Saskatchewan food producers and businesses, and have an in-house restaurant, Meld Eatery, where they also make ready-made meals.

SaskMade Marketplace

1621 8th Street East, Saskatoon, SK S7H 0T2 and Midtown Plaza (second floor)
201 1st Avenue South, Saskatoon SK S7K 1J9 / (306) 955-1832 / saskmade.ca
»The name says it all. SaskMade is a retail outlet that partners with local farmers and producers to offer both grocery and artisanal products. Their storefronts are both located in Saskatoon, and they deliver within Saskatoon and to Regina. You can also order through their online store.

The Wandering Market

461 Athabasca St East, Moose Jaw, SK S6H 0L9 / (306) 690-3553 / thewanderingmarket.com
»The Wandering Market stocks goods from Saskatchewan producers, growers, and artisans province-wide. They have an in-store market in Moose Jaw and also deliver to Moose Jaw, Kindersley, Saskatoon, Regina, Swift Current, and the surrounding areas. See their website for delivery details and a full list of surrounding area delivery locations.

Flat Out Delicious: Your Definitive Guide to Saskatchewan's Food Artisans by Jenn Sharp (TouchWood Editions, 2020) is also an excellent resource if you are looking for information on food producers and growers province-wide, and provides comprehensive information on more than 150 food artisans in Saskatchewan.

Disclaimer: The information in this guide was accurate at time of writing. If you are making a trip somewhere for a specific or seasonal ingredient, call ahead to ensure they have what you need.

Note: For some of the listed locations, especially farms or orchards, I have not included a specific address and instead noted only the city/town and postal code. This is because many rural businesses do not have a formal street address. If you are trying to visit a certain location and enter the name into a GPS, directions should come up. If you need more information, contact the business directly or visit their website.

With Gratitude

Writing my first book has been a memorable experience, one that still seems almost too good to be true at times. I am endlessly thankful for the opportunity to pursue a creative profession, knowing that every challenging moment is balanced by an encouraging one and that the rewards are infinite.

In the early stages of my time working on *Only in Saskatchewan* someone made a comment likening this book to a massive group project, and I can't help but agree. A book like this does not materialize without the support of numerous people, all of whom played a significant role in the process.

It is with enormous gratitude that I extend a thank you to all the business owners, chefs, bakers, cooks, and staff who agreed to come along for this journey. Without you, this book simply would not exist. Thank you for being excited about this project and its potential. Thank you for sharing your coveted recipes, welcoming me into your kitchens, and putting up with my constant emails and questions—we all know there were a lot of them. I will always be grateful for your time, effort, and contributions.

Thank you to Garrett Kendel, who brought *Only in Saskatchewan* to life in ways far beyond anything I had ever imagined. Garrett, your photography is brilliant and gives these recipes and places the vibrancy they deserve. Thank you for your dedication to this project and for being patient about my particularity. I am truly in awe of your work and the finished product.

To the TouchWood Editions team: your commitment and care has shown me that I've truly hit the jackpot in the publisher lottery. Taryn Boyd, thank you for believing in this book from the beginning and for walking me through the publishing process. You have been patient with my millions of questions, and I so appreciate that you appreciate a good question list. Thank you to Tori Elliott, Kate Kennedy, Curtis Samuel, Lesley Cameron, Sydney Barnes, Paula Marchese, and Tree Abraham—you are all an absolute dream team to work with. A special thanks to Tori and Kate for continuing to be patient with my question lists along the way. And to Lesley: I'm pretty sure your editing wizardry shaved about 15 pages off this book—thank you for your expertise and kindness thoughout the process.

Thank you to SK Arts and Tourism Saskatchewan, whose generosity helped make *Only in Saskatchewan* possible. To SK Arts: your support meant I could focus solely on research and writing for months on end, which allowed me to fully immerse myself in my work. To Tourism Saskatchewan: your support enabled Garrett and me to travel and visit all of the establishments featured here. To both: your support helped make this book what it is. Thank you.

A special thanks to Jacqueline Ottmann, Keighlagh Donovan, Melody Wood, and Stryker Calvez for your insights and review of the Land Acknowledgment.

Thank you to everyone who volunteered their time and energy to test and retest recipes: Aimee Carreiro, Archer Bell, Aunya Zurevinski, Ellen May-Melin, Elyse Hamp, Emma Bugg, Gail May-Melin, Janis Brahniuk, Jazlyn Perehudoff, Jeff May-Melin, Keighlagh Donovan, Luke Hansen, Lynette Epp, Matt Barwick, Michelle MacGowan, Paul Hansen, Renée Boechler, Rick Brahniuk, Ron Zurevinski, Sandy Zurevinski, Sheila Baribeau, and Stephanie Mah. To all of you: your help was crucial in freeing up my time for writing and editing. I am so appreciative of your comments and observations, which ensured the recipes were ready for publication. From the bottom of my heart, thank you.

Thank you to everyone who provided suggestions about which establishments should be included. A special thanks to Allan Pulga, Jenn Sharp, Kevin Dunn, and Ashlyn George for their ideas. A special thanks to Rebecca Wellman for sharing your experiences with writing *First, We Brunch: Recipes and Stories from Victoria's Best-Loved Breakfast Joints*. I flipped through *First, We Brunch* many a time throughout the process. A special thanks also to Amy Jo Ehman, for assistance on grant writing and for providing advice on the book writing process. I printed off that email with the advice and read it repeatedly, especially in the final weeks when I needed encouragement most.

To Jacque and Mike Zinkowski and family, Luke and Jaz, and Janis and Rick: thank you for watching our little pup on days when I was on the road. It was reassuring to know she was in good hands.

To Keighlagh: thank you for your help on multiple aspects of the manuscript. Your edits have been insightful and thorough since our days at *the Sheaf*, and I so appreciate you and your feedback.

To Steph: thank you for reviewing early elements of the book and for always understanding the challenges that come with creative work. You are a kindred spirit in work and life.

To Ellen: thank you for your thoughts and review of multiple elements of the manuscript. You have been a constant and true friend to me for years, and I'm so grateful for you.

Thank you to all the family and friends who dropped off food and checked in on me, especially in the final weeks of writing. I am so lucky to be surrounded by loved ones who have supported me from day one. A special thanks to Janis and Rick, Luke and Jaz, and Yvonne and Lorne Nelson for your love and support.

Thank you to my grandparents, Sylvia and Glen Zolotarchuk and Anne Zurevinski: you've been at every recital and performance since I was young, and I know I can count on you three to read every word I write. I love you all.

To my parents, Ron and Sandy Zurevinski: you have always encouraged me in my pursuit of an unconventional career, and granting Aunya and me the freedom to pursue creative work is perhaps one of the greatest gifts you gave us. This freedom has given me the confidence to explore and try new things without fear. Thank you for your unconditional support, for being enthusiastic about everything I do, and for always showing up, even if it's with a video camera in tow. I love you both very much.

To my sister Aunya: you shine so brightly, and it reminds me to smile more and not take myself so seriously. Thank you for being both my sister and my best friend. I love you dearly, Little Ray.

And finally, to my husband, Paul: I cannot say thank you enough. We both know this never would have come together had it not been for your unwavering love. Thank you for encouraging me to submit the book proposal in the first place, for talking through every aspect of the book with me, for editing the entire manuscript (even if sometimes I was grumpy about your edits, I admit they were correct), and for cleaning up the kitchen after I was done testing recipes. Most of all, thank you for always being there, on good days and bad, and for believing in me every step of the way. You challenge me to be a better writer and a better version of myself, and I am eternally grateful for that. I love you.

Bibliography

"About Thai Select." Thai Select. thaiselect.ca/about

"Alvin Scheresky." Daybreak Mill. daybreakmill.com/blogs/who-we-are/alvin-scheresky

"Bakeries & Confectionaries." PDF. Courtesy of Melfort & District Museum. melfortmuseum.org/

"Block 9 Lot 13A." Word Document. Courtesy of Melfort & District Museum. melfortmuseum.org/

"Clean Food & All Natural Meat." Pine View Farms. pineviewfarms.com/pages/clean-food-all-natural-meat

"FAQ." Office of the Treaty Commissioner. otc.ca/pages/faq

"Land Titles Office Building." City of Moose Jaw. moosejaw.ca/heritage_properties/land-titles-office-building/

Mohammed, Farah. "Who Was La Malinche?" JSTOR Daily. daily.jstor.org/who-was-la-malinche/

"Our Building." Yvette Moore Gallery. yvettemoore.com/our-building/

"Our Farm." Bison Ridge Farms. bisonridgefarms.com/

"Our Story." Black Fox Farm & Distillery. blackfoxfarmanddistillery.com/our-story/

"Our Story." Boreal Heartland. borealheartland.ca/pages/about-us

"Our Story." Pine View Farms. pineviewfarms.com/pages/our-story

"Our Story." Yvette Moore Gallery. yvettemoore.com/our-story/

"Rosthern Canadian National Railway Station." Canada's Historic Places. Parks Canada. historicplaces.ca/en/rep-reg/place-lieu.aspx?id=5676

Walker, Ernie. "Our Story." Wanuskewin Heritage Park. wanuskewin.com/our-story/

"What is the Boreal Forest?" Boreal Heartland. borealheartland.ca/pages/what-is-the-boreal-forest

"Who We Are." Daybreak Mill. daybreakmill.com/pages/about-us

Wolvengrey, Arok (ed.). *Plains Cree Dictionary*. Volume 1: Cree-English and Volume 2: English-Cree. dictionary.plainscree.atlas-ling.ca

"Yvette's Story." Yvette Moore Gallery. yvettemoore.com/yvettemoore/

Archival Photo Credits

Page 57 (Golden Grain Bakery): Melfort & District Museum.

Page 64 (Station Arts Centre): University of Saskatchewan, University Archives & Special Collections, Keith Ewart fonds MG 259, Rosthern Station Postcard.

Page 80 (Rawhides Bistro and Saloon): Supplied by Bob Koroluk, via stenensask.com.

Page 98 (Danish Home Bakery): From the Thiell family's personal photographs.

Page 122 (Baba's Perogies): Saskatoon Public Library, Local History Photograph Collection QC-4597-1.

Page 142 (Wanuskewin): Supplied by Wanuskewin.

Page 164 (Calories): City of Saskatoon Archives—1003-444.

Page 206 (Houston Pizza): Roy Antal / *Regina Leader-Post*, a division of Postmedia Network Inc.

Page 246 (Yvette Moore Gallery): Moose Jaw Public Library Archives Department, Lewis Rice Collection.

Index

Metric Conversion Chart

VOLUME

Imperial	Metric
⅛ tsp	0.5 mL
¼ tsp	1 mL
½ tsp	2.5 mL
¾ tsp	4 mL
1 tsp	5 mL
½ Tbsp	8 mL
1 Tbsp	15 mL
1½ Tbsp	23 mL
2 Tbsp	30 mL
2½ Tbsp	38 mL
¼ cup	60 mL
⅓ cup	80 mL
½ cup	125 mL
⅔ cup	165 mL
¾ cup	185 mL
1 cup	250 mL
1¼ cups	310 mL
1⅓ cups	330 mL
1½ cups	375 mL
1⅔ cups	415 mL
1¾ cups	435 mL
2 cups / 1 pint	500 mL
2¼ cups	560 mL
2⅓ cups	580 mL
2½ cups	625 mL
2⅔ cups	665 mL
2¾ cups	690 mL
3 cups	750 mL
3½ cups	875 mL
4 cups	1 L
5 cups	1.25 L
6 cups	1.5 L
8 cups / 2 quarts	2 L
25 cups	6 L

WEIGHT

Imperial	Metric
1 oz	30 g
4 oz	115 g
8 oz	225 g
10 oz	250 g
12 oz	340 g
1 lb (16 oz)	450 g
2 lb	900 g
5 lb	2,250 g

CANS

Imperial	Metric
6 oz	177mL
10 oz	284 mL
11oz	300ml
14 oz	398 mL
16 oz	480 mL
28 oz	796 mL

LENGTH/WIDTH

Imperial	Metric
¹⁄₁₂ inch	2 mm
⅛ inch	3 mm
⅙ inch	4 mm
¼ inch	6 mm
½ inch	12 mm
¾ inch	2 cm
1 inch	2.5 cm
1½ inches	3.5 cm
2 inches	5 cm
2½ inches	6.5 cm
3 inches	7.5 cm
3½ inches	9 cm
4 inches	10 cm
5 inches	12.5 cm
6 inches	15 cm
7 inches	18 cm
8 inches	20 cm
9 inches	23 cm
10 inches	25 cm

TEMPERATURE

(For oven temperatures, see chart below)

Imperial	Metric
115°F	46°C
150°F	66°C
160°F	71°C
170°F	77°C
180°F	82°C
185°F	85°C
190°F	88°C
200°F	93°C
240°F	116°C
247°F	119°C
250°F	121°C
290°F	143°C
300°F	149°C
350°F	177°C
360°F	182°C
370°F	188°C

OVEN TEMPERATURE

Imperial	Metric
200°F	95°C
225°F	105°C
250°F	120°C
275°F	135°C
300°F	150°C
325°F	160°C
350°F	180°C
375°F	190°C
400°F	200°C
425°F	220°C
450°F	230°C

US FLUID OUNCES

US fluid ounces	US customary	Metric
¼ oz	½ Tbsp / 1½ tsp	7.5 mL
⅓ oz	2 tsp	10 mL
½ oz	1 Tbsp	15 mL
¾ oz	1½ Tbsp / 4½ tsp	22 mL
1 oz (1 shot)	2 Tbsp	30 mL
1¼ oz	2½ Tbsp	37.5 mL
1½ oz	3 Tbsp	45 mL
2 oz	¼ cup	60 mL
2½ oz	5 Tbsp	75 mL
3 oz	¼ cup + 2 Tbsp	90 mL
3½ oz	¼ cup + 3 Tbsp	105 mL
4 oz	½ cup	125 mL
4½ oz	½ cup + 1 Tbsp	140 mL
5 oz	½ cup + 2 Tbsp	155 mL

© Harrison Hall

GARRETT KENDEL is a Saskatoon-based photographer, videographer, and certified drone operator. He launched King Rose Visuals in 2019, and since then has worked with clients across Canada, with a focus on architecture, design, and small businesses.

kingrosevisuals.com
@kingrosevisuals